Credits

Acquisitions Editor
Aaron Black

Project Editor
Jade L. Williams

Technical Editor
Dennis Cohen

Copy Editor
Scott Tullis

Editorial Director
Robyn Siesky

Business Manager
Amy Knies

Senior Marketing Manager
Sandy Smith

**Vice President and Executive
Group Publisher**
Richard Swadley

**Vice President and Executive
Publisher**
Barry Pruett

Project Coordinator
Sheree Montgomery

Graphics and Production Specialists
Andrea Hornberger
Sennett V. Johnson
Sarah Wright

Quality Control Technician
Rebecca Denoncour

Proofreading
The Well-Chosen Word

Indexing
BIM Indexing & Proofreading Services

About the Author

Ben Harvell is a freelance writer based in Bournemouth, U.K., writing for a range of international technology magazines including *Macworld, Macformat, MacLife,* and *MacUser*. He also provides scriptwriting for commercials and web videos to tech startups and other established brands.

Formerly the editor of *iCreate Magazine*, Ben is the author of several consumer technology books including *Make Music with your iPad* and is never far from the latest consumer tech or social media platforms.

When time allows he blogs at www.benharvell.com but is more often found on Twitter (@benharvell) and, of course, Facebook at www.facebook.com/benharvelldotcom.

Author's Acknowledgments

I joined Facebook on January 23, 2007 on the advice of my sister (someone I rarely listen to), who claimed that it was "the next big thing." Five years, several UI changes, privacy disputes, an IPO, and this book later, I have to admit — she was right. Congratulations, Amelia Harvell, you made it onto the Acknowledgments page.

I'd also like to thank Aaron Black and his excellent team at Wiley for continuing to make the books I write look and sound better than I could imagine. Special thanks go to Jade Williams for a steadfast dedication to quality and accuracy and the patience of a saint. Without her, this book would probably be called *Teach Yourself Verbally: Freebook* and be littered with my off-topic rambling. It's rare the queen of England hands out knighthoods to those outside the commonwealth, but I'm adding Jade to the list. Dennis Cohen should also be highlighted, not only for having an incredible tech mind and providing eagle-eyed fact checking, but also for keeping me entertained and motivated during the long writing hours with exceptionally witty comments added to my copy.

To the behind the scenes crew, spotting my "Briticisms," tweaking my spelling, and making sense of my screenshots, I salute you.

Finally, I suppose it's only fitting to thank the team behind Facebook. Yes, you did introduce Timeline to the platform right in the middle of my book, but, throughout writing it, I have been constantly surprised and excited by the many great features and slick technology that Facebook offers. The world would be a different place, for good and for bad, without it and that's the kind of dent in history that I like to see made.

Teach Yourself VISUALLY™

Facebook®

Visual

by Ben Harvell

Teach Yourself VISUALLY™ Facebook®

Published by
John Wiley & Sons, Inc.
10475 Crosspoint Boulevard
Indianapolis, IN 46256

www.wiley.com

Published simultaneously in Canada

Copyright © 2012 by John Wiley & Sons, Inc., Indianapolis, Indiana

Wiley publishes in a variety of print and electronic formats and by print-on-demand. Some material included with standard print versions of this book may not be included in e-books or in print-on-demand. If this book refers to media such as a CD or DVD that is not included in the version you purchased, you may download this material at http://booksupport.wiley.com. For more information about Wiley products, visit www.wiley.com.

Library of Congress Control Number: 2012948656

ISBN: 978-1-118-37488-7

Manufactured in the United States of America

10 9 8 7 6 5 4 3 2 1

Trademark Acknowledgments

Contact Us

For general information on our other products and services please contact our Customer Care Department within the U.S. at 877-762-2974, outside the U.S. at 317-572-3993 or fax 317-572-4002.

For technical support please visit www.wiley.com/techsupport.

WILEY **Sales** | Contact Wiley at (877) 762-2974 or fax (317) 572-4002.

How to Use This Book

Who This Book Is For

This book is for the reader who has never used this particular technology or software application. It is also for readers who want to expand their knowledge.

The Conventions in This Book

① Steps

This book uses a step-by-step format to guide you easily through each task. **Numbered steps** are actions you must do; **bulleted steps** clarify a point, step, or optional feature; and **indented steps** give you the result.

② Notes

Notes give additional information — special conditions that may occur during an operation, a situation that you want to avoid, or a cross-reference to a related area of the book.

③ Icons and Buttons

Icons and buttons show you exactly what you need to click to perform a step.

④ Tips

Tips offer additional information, including warnings and shortcuts.

⑤ Bold

Bold type shows command names or options that you must click or text or numbers you must type.

⑥ Italics

Italic type introduces and defines a new term.

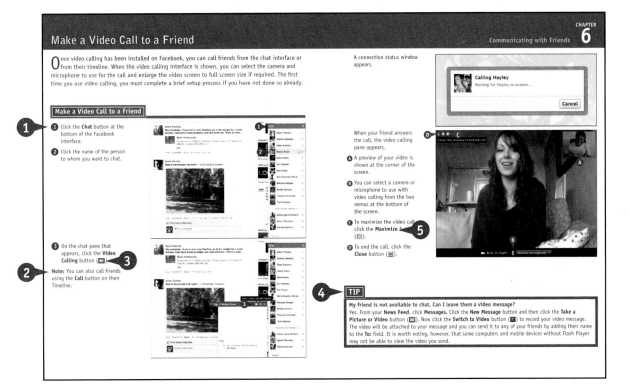

Table of Contents

Chapter 3 Setting Privacy

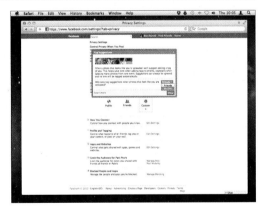

Table of Contents

Chapter 6	Communicating with Friends

Table of Contents

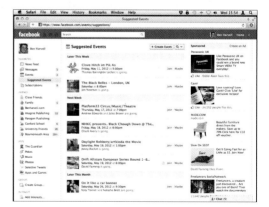

| Chapter 9 | Sharing Photos, Video, and Music |

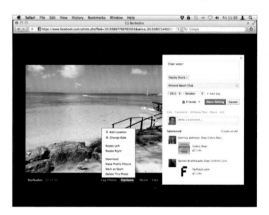

Table of Contents

Chapter 12 | Using Search and Notifications

Table of Contents

Chapter 15   Understanding Facebook Ads and Pages

CHAPTER 1

Setting Up an Account

You get started on Facebook by creating a new account, building your profile, and finding friends to add to your network. This includes adding details about your job, religious beliefs, and activities you enjoy. You can also add contact information to help friends get in touch, and add a profile picture so you are more easily recognizable on Facebook.

Introducing the Facebook Interface

Facebook provides a common layout across its pages, making it easy to navigate between sections of your account. The Facebook interface is split into three distinct columns, with the main content of a page appearing in the center. Navigation links appear on the left of the interface, and advertising, recommendations, and the chat menu are on the right. Across the top of the Facebook interface, you can access notification menus and links to account settings as well as a search box. When your browser window is maximized or wide enough, a news ticker and the full chat interface is shown as a fourth column.

The Facebook News Feed

The Facebook News Feed is the first view you see when logging in to your account. The News Feed shows activity from all your Facebook friends including status updates, comments, and uploaded photos and videos.

On the left side of the page is a column of links to different sections of your Facebook account such as Messages, Events, Apps, and Lists.

The right of the page is dedicated to event and birthday notifications among others, plus friend suggestions and sponsored links. Dragging the browser window wider shows the Facebook ticker and full Chat interface. Ticker shows recent comments and status updates from your friends.

The Facebook Timeline

Your Facebook timeline is shown when you click your name on the left of the Facebook window and is visible to your friends depending on your privacy settings. The timeline shows a chronologically ordered list of events in your life including status updates, photos, friends, and app information. The timeline automatically adds what it believes are relevant events in your life, and you can add your own cover image to your Facebook timeline as well as add additional significant events you choose in a variety of categories, such as Life Events, Photos and employment details. The timeline is designed so that friends can view a complete history of your life from birth through education, jobs, and family-related matters such as births and marriages. Changes to your profile picture and shared links and images are also included in your timeline. You are free to hide elements on your timeline if you want.

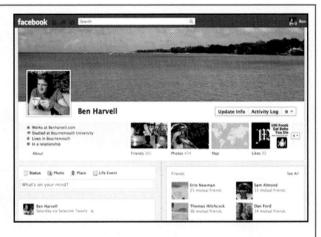

Facebook Messages

The Messages interface is a central hub for all messages you have sent and received on Facebook. From this screen you can write a new message, reply to messages you have been sent and search through previous conversations. The search box enables you to search within particular message criteria such as unread messages, archived messages, sent messages, and spam. Clicking a message on this page shows all sent and received messages within that particular conversation and enables you to write another message to that person. You can also archive or mark as unread any message on the main Messages screen by clicking the buttons next to the message. When you sign up for Facebook Email, all your e-mails appear on this screen, enabling you to search and read as regular Facebook messages.

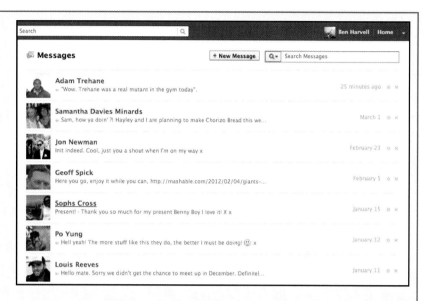

Facebook Photos

Clicking Photos on the left-hand column on Facebook shows you all photos and videos uploaded by your friends as well as your own in chronological order. You can also see all the comments on each image and comment or Like them yourself by using the links below each image. From this page, you can create new photo albums to share with your friends, and upload photos and videos to your Facebook page by clicking the relevant buttons at the top of the interface. The **+ Upload Photos** and **+ Upload Video** buttons open a browser window within which you can select photos or videos from your computer's hard drive to upload to Facebook. Clicking **My Albums** takes you to a page that includes photos and videos you have previously uploaded as well as photos in which you have been tagged.

Create an Account

To create a Facebook account, you must visit www.facebook.com via your web browser or the official Facebook app for iOS and Android. Here you will find an option to create a new account by typing your name, e-mail address, and a password into the required fields. You will also be asked to include your sex and birth date. This information is used as your login details and also to make sure that you have not used this address with Facebook before. If the Facebook system recognizes your e-mail address, you are asked to login instead of set up a new account.

Create an Account

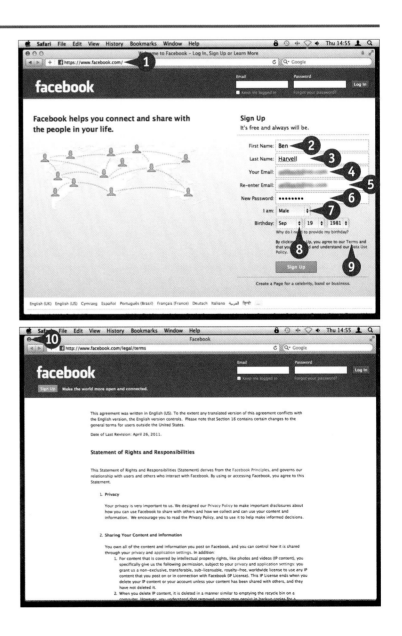

1. Type **www.facebook.com** into your browser's address bar and press `Enter` (`Return`) to visit the Facebook welcome page.

2. Type your first name.

3. Type your last name.

4. Type your e-mail address.

5. Retype your e-mail address.

6. Type a password and then type it again in the next field to confirm it.

7. Click the **I am** arrow (⬍) and select your sex from the pop-up menu.

8. Click the **Birthday** arrow (⬍) and select your birth month, date, and year from the pop-up menus.

9. Click **Terms** to read the terms of the Data Use Policy.

   The Terms page opens in a new tab or browser window.

10. Click **Close** (⬛) to return to the Sign Up page.

11 Click **Sign Up**.

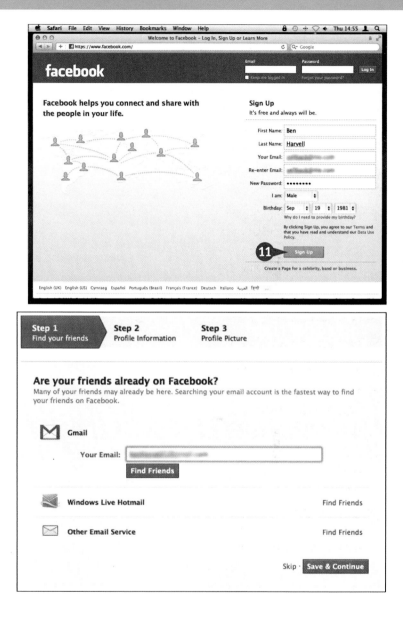

Facebook creates your
account and takes you to
the Find Friends page.

TIP

As a small-business owner, is creating a Facebook account the right option for me?
A basic Facebook account is designed for personal use only, so that a single user can contact friends and
share photos. However, once you have created your personal account, you can create a Facebook page for a
business, band, or public figure. This is an ideal tool for promoting a brand and can be managed via your
personal Facebook account.

Find Friends

The first step in the three-step Facebook account creation process is to find friends who are already using Facebook and invite those who are not. By accessing contacts from your e-mail accounts, including Hotmail and Yahoo!, Facebook detects those already using Facebook and enables you to e-mail invitations to those who are not. Facebook requires your e-mail address and password to access your contacts but does not send invites until you select and approve those you want. You are free to skip this option if you do not wish to use your contacts with Facebook.

Find Friends

1 Click **Find Friends** next to the account type in which you want to search.

2 Type your e-mail address for the account in the **Your Email:** field.

3 Click **Find Friends**.

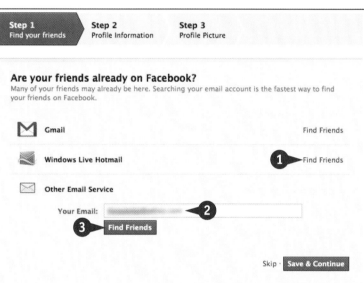

A login window for your e-mail account appears.

4 Type the username for your e-mail account.

5 Type a password.

6 Click **Sign In**.

Note: Different e-mail accounts may require additional login information or show different login screens.

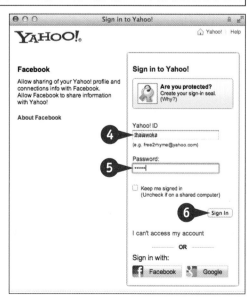

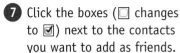

7 Click the boxes (☐ changes to ☑) next to the contacts you want to add as friends.

8 Click **Add Friends**.

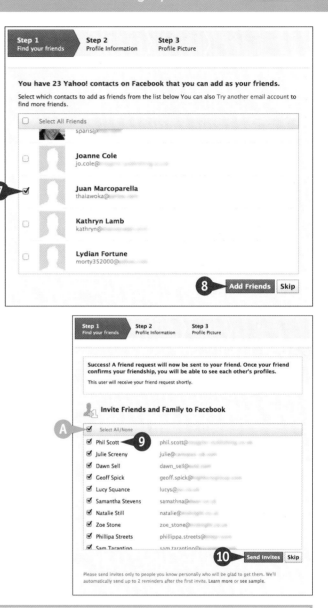

9 Click the boxes (☐ changes to ☑) next to friends in your contacts you want to invite to Facebook.

10 Click **Send Invites**.

Ⓐ You can choose to select all available contacts to invite to Facebook by checking this box (☐ changes to ☑).

Do I have to search for contacts on Facebook?

No. You can skip this step by clicking the **Skip** link or **Skip** buttons to move to the next step in your account setup. You can then choose to search for friends after your account has been set up. Friends can also find you when your account is live and invite you to become friends.

Why do I not see any available contacts when searching my e-mail account?

Facebook looks for e-mail addresses linked to Facebook accounts. If none of your contacts is using Facebook, none of them appears in this search. You can, however, invite the contacts found in this search to join Facebook by sending them an e-mail. If you would rather avoid sending mail from Facebook, you can use your existing e-mail account.

Create a Profile

Adding information about your school, university, and workplace helps you to find friends already using Facebook. The second step of the Facebook account setup process enables you to enter your work information as well as the years you were in school in order to find friends that attended the same school at the same time. This information is not required to complete the account setup process, but will help you locate people to add as friends without the need to search for them. That said, depending on class numbers and enrollment figures for your school year, searching may still be a better option when looking for specific friends to connect with.

Create a Profile

1 Click in the **High School** field and begin typing the name of your high school.

2 From the list that appears, select your high school.

If your high school is not listed, continue typing the full name.

3 Click the **High School** arrow (⊡) and select the year you finished high school from the pop-up menu.

4 Click in the **College/University** field and type the name of your college.

5 Click the **College/University** arrow (⬍) and select the year you finished college from the pop-up menu.

6 Click in the **Employer** field and type your current employer.

7 Click **Save & Continue**.

8 Click **+1 Add Friend** next to the people Facebook suggests that you want to add as friends.

9 Click **Save & Continue**.

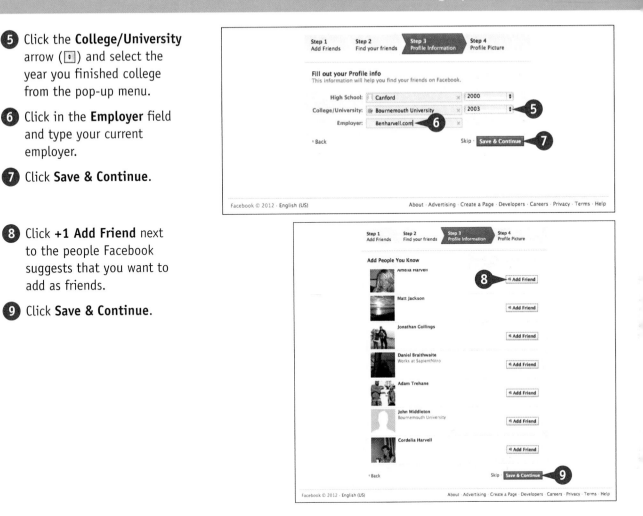

How do I remove incorrect information?
If you want to remove information entered for your high school, college, university, or employer you can click the **X** next to its name to remove it. You can then retype the information into the required field to correct your mistake or leave it blank.

How can I skip the profile information step?
You can click the **Skip** link next to the Save & Continue button to move to the next step. You can always edit your profile information after your account has been created by going to the Edit Profile screen. From here, you can add new details or remove information you added previously.

Add a Profile Picture

To personalize your account and help friends find you on Facebook, you can add a profile picture as the third step of the account setup. You can upload the picture from your computer or take one using your webcam. If you prefer to add a photo later, you may skip this step for now. You are free to change your profile picture at any time after you have set up your Facebook account. If you choose not to add a profile picture at this stage, Facebook uses the default blue and white silhouette image.

Add a Profile Picture

1 Click the **Upload a Photo** link.

The Profile Picture window appears.

2 Click **Choose File**.

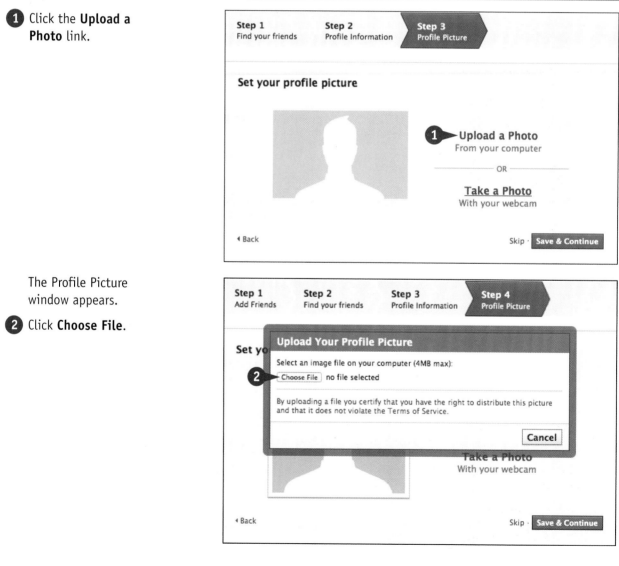

The folder directory window appears.

3 Locate and select the file on your computer that you want to use as a profile picture from the browser window that appears.

4 Click **Choose**.

5 Check your picture in the preview area and click **Save & Continue**.

Note: If you are not happy with the image you have uploaded, you can click the **Remove Your Picture** link below the image.

TIP

How do I take a profile picture with my webcam?
Follow these steps:

1 Click the **Take a Photo** link.

Note: If an Adobe Flash Player Settings box appears, click the **Allow** option and click **Close**. You may be required to install Flash to use this feature. Flash will not work on iOS devices, so iPhone, iPad and iPod touch users must use the Facebook app for their device in order to take and upload pictures.

2 Pose for the picture in front of your webcam and click the **Camera** button () to take the photo.

3 Click **Save Picture**.

4 Click **Save & Continue**.

Validate Your E-Mail Address

Once the Facebook account setup process is complete, you must perform one final step to authorize the account. An e-mail is sent to the address you signed up with and includes a link that must be clicked to validate the e-mail address for use with the Facebook account. If the e-mail is not validated, you will be allowed only limited access to your Facebook account. The e-mail is sent as soon as you complete the basic setup process and includes instructions on how to validate your e-mail address. If you cannot find the e-mail, check your Junk mailbox to see if it has been marked as spam.

Validate Your E-Mail Address

1 Check your e-mail account for an e-mail from Facebook.

2 Open the e-mail and click the link to validate your e-mail address.

Note: If you cannot find the e-mail that Facebook sent, click the **Resend Email** button at the top of the Facebook interface.

Your account signup is now complete.

3 Click **Okay**.

Facebook reappears in your browser.

Log into Your Account

To access Facebook from your computer, you need to log in via the web interface. This requires the e-mail address you signed up with and the password you set during signup. You can find the login section at the top of the page at www.facebook.com. Links are available to help you access your details if you happen to forget them. You must visit this page each time you log in to Facebook, and you can set the login page to remember your e-mail address for a quicker sign-in process.

Log into Your Account

1 Type **www.facebook. com** into your browser's URL bar and press Enter (Return).

2 Type your e-mail address into the **Email** field at the top of the screen.

3 Type your password into the **Password** field at the top of the screen.

4 Click **Log In**.

A Click the **Keep me logged in** box (☐ changes to ☑) if you want your browser to remember your e-mail address.

Enter Your Basic Information

You can find the basic information section when you opt to edit your profile. This section includes information concerning your location, age, and sex as well as other basic details. By default, this information will be visible to everyone; however, you can set different privacy settings for each piece of information to determine who can see it when people view your profile. See the Tip section for how to do this using the **Audience Selector**. Information added here can help people find you, and Facebook uses it in different ways. For example, if you choose to display your birth date on your profile, your friends are notified when your birthday is near.

Enter Your Basic Information

1 Log in to your account and click your name at the top right of the interface.

2 Click **Update Info**.

The Update Info screen appears.

3 Click **Edit** next to Basic Info.

4 Click the **I Am** arrow (▢) and select your sex from the pop-up menu.

5 Click the **Birthday** arrows (▢) and select your birth month, date, and year from the pop-up menus.

6 Select the sex in which you are interested (☐ changes to ☑).

Note: The information you add to this section can easily be made private using the **Audience Selector** (🔽) to the right of each field. You can make the information only visible to you or only to friends.

7 Type any languages you know into the **Languages** field.

8 Click **Save**.

Ⓐ Your information is added to your profile.

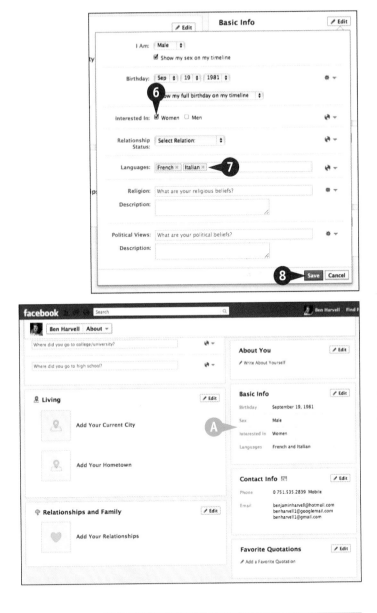

How do I set who can view my basic profile information?
By default, your basic profile information appears to everyone with whom you are friends. The Audience Selector menu (🔽) appears next to each section of information on the Basic Information page. You can set who can view your profile information by clicking the 🔽 and then clicking a different privacy setting from the menu that appears.

Add Friends and Family Information

Editing friends and family information on your profile enables you to set which of your contacts you are related to or you are in a relationship with. The page also shows the number of Facebook friends you have. Setting your relationship status allows you to choose a Facebook friend with whom you are in a relationship and determine the level of that relationship, be it engaged, married, or simply dating. You can also set which of your Facebook friends are also members of your family and define their relationship to you.

Add Friends and Family Information

1 Click your name at the top right of the interface.

2 Click **Update Info**.

The Update Info screen appears.

3 Click **Edit** next to Relationships and Family.

4 Click the **Relationship Status** arrow ( ) and select the type of relationship you are in from the pop-up menu.

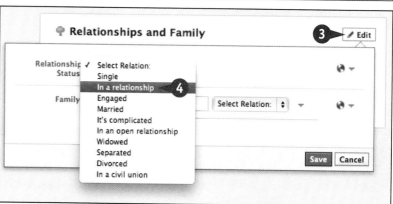

5 Type the name of your partner in the **with** field.

Note: If you choose Single from the **Relationship Status** pop-up menu, you cannot select a partner.

Note: If your partner is on Facebook and connected as a friend, you can select his or her name from the pop-up menu that appears.

Note: If you select a person on Facebook who you are in a relationship with, you can also set an anniversary date from the pop-up menus that appear.

6 Type the name of a Family member.

7 Click the **Family** arrow (⬍) and select the person's relation to you from the pop-up menu.

8 Click the **Add another family member** link to add more members of your family.

9 Click **Save**.

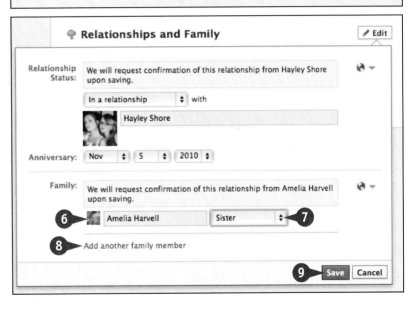

Why is my relationship status not showing up on my profile?
The Facebook friend you have selected as the person you are in a relationship with needs to confirm that you are in a relationship before it can be shown on your profile page.

Who can see my relationship and family information?
By default, your relationship status and family information is public, but you can change the privacy settings for each by clicking the Audience Selector menu (⬍) to the right of each section on this page.

Add Work and Education Information

The Education and Work section of your profile shows where you have worked, where you currently work, and the school and universities at which you studied. Within the work and education categories, you can enter multiple institutions and more specific options such as projects worked on and classes you attended. This information can help friends and work colleagues find you on Facebook and help you increase the number of Facebook friends you have.

Add Work and Education Information

1 Click your name at the top right of the interface.

2 Click **Update Info**.

The Update Info screen appears.

3 Click **Edit** next to Work and Education.

4 Type a company where you have worked in the **Where have you worked?** field.

5 Fill in your employment information — your position at the company, its location, and your job description.

6 Click the **I currently work here** option (☐ changes to ☑), or click the **Year** arrow (⬚) and the **+ Add month** link to set the time of your employment.

7 Click **Add Job**.

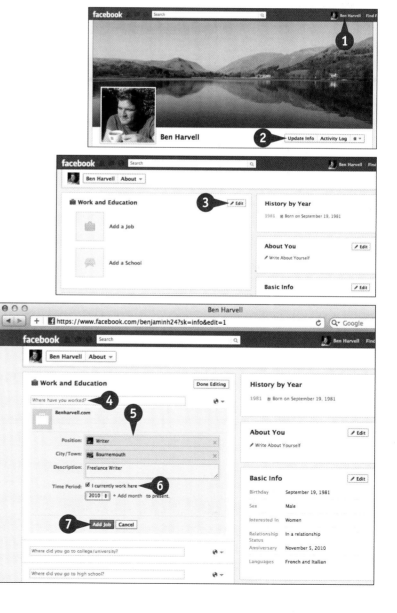

20

8 Type the name of your college or university into the **College/University** field.

9 Click the **Time Period** arrows (⊡) and the **+ Add month** links to set the start and end time of your education.

10 Click the **Graduated** option if applicable (☐ changes to ☑) and type the degree earned.

11 Fill in your education and its focus.

12 Click a **College** or **Graduate School** option (☐ changes to ⊙).

If you select **Graduate School,** you can enter a degree type.

13 Click **Add School**.

14 Type your high school name into the **High School** field.

Note: You can continue to type high school names to add more than one if required.

15 Click the **Time Period** arrows (⊡) and the **+ Add month** links to select the start and end date of your attendance.

16 Click the **Graduated** option if applicable (☐ changes to ☑) and add a description of your focus.

17 Click **Add School**.

TIP

What do the project and class links do?
Below your employment and education information, you can click the **Add a Project** or **Add a Class** links. These links enable you to add more detailed information such as specific projects you worked on or classes you attended. You can also select friends you worked or studied with and provide a description.

Add Religious and Political Information

The Basic Info sections of your profile show your religious and political views. You can enter any religion or political view you want, or select any of the recommendations that appear on a list as you type. You can then add a description for each to further explain your views. This information can be made public, private to you, or only visible to your friends, using the Audience Selector. It is not a requirement to enter political or religious information on your profile, so you can leave this section blank if you wish.

Add Religious and Political Information

1 Click your name at the top right of the interface.

2 Click **Update Info**.

The Update Info screen appears

3 Click **Edit** next to Basic Info.

4 Type your religion in the **Religion** field.

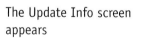

5 From the list that appears, click a religion from the menu that pops up as you type.

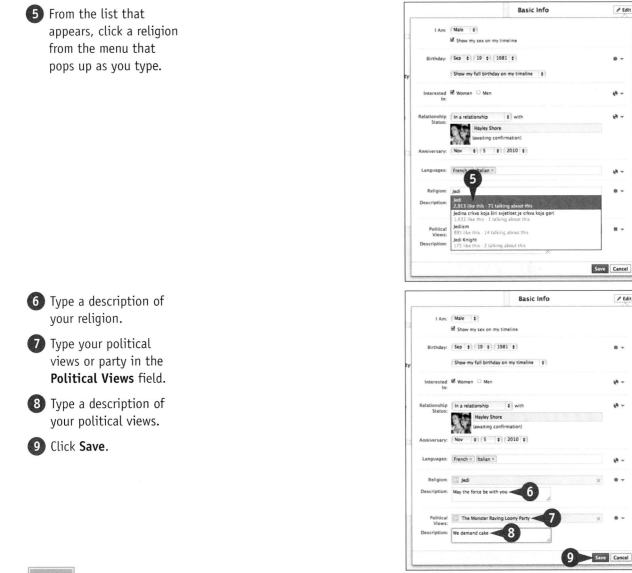

6 Type a description of your religion.

7 Type your political views or party in the **Political Views** field.

8 Type a description of your political views.

9 Click **Save**.

Where will people see this information?

Depending on the privacy settings you have set, the details you add here are visible when visitors click the **Info** link on your profile. You can adjust your privacy settings so that only close friends or family members can see this information. If there is information added to your profile that you do not want displayed publicly, you should either remove it or set your privacy settings accordingly using the Audience Selector for each piece of information you do not want to share.

Add an E-Mail Account

As well as the account you used to sign up to Facebook, you can include additional e-mail addresses on your profile. These e-mail addresses are then shown under the Info section of your profile page, and depending on your privacy settings, offer Facebook friends an alternate way to contact you. You can add e-mail addresses for your work or home. When adding e-mail accounts, you can set whether or not friends can download your e-mail address when they use the Download Your Information feature to store their Facebook information on their computer.

Add an E-Mail Account

1 Click the **Account** menu (▾).

2 Click **Account Settings**.

The General Account Settings window opens.

3 Click **Edit** on the Email section.

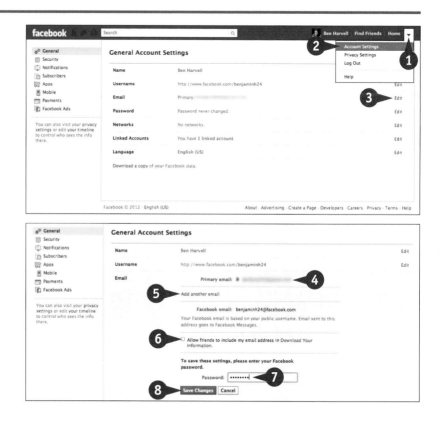

4 Select your primary e-mail account (☐ changes to ◉).

5 Click **Add another email** to add a new e-mail account.

6 Click this option (☐ changes to ☑) to allow friends to download your e-mail address.

7 Type your password.

8 Click **Save Changes**.

Add Telephone Numbers and Address Information

Y ou can add additional contact information to your Facebook account including your home or work phone number and address details on the Contact Information screen. Here you can include your work and home landline numbers, as well as any other landline numbers that you want to share. Mobile phone numbers should be used in the Mobile Phones section of the Contact Information settings, but you can enter a mobile phone number on this screen if you want to.

Add Telephone Numbers and Address Information

1 Click your name at the top right of the screen.

2 Click **Update Info**.

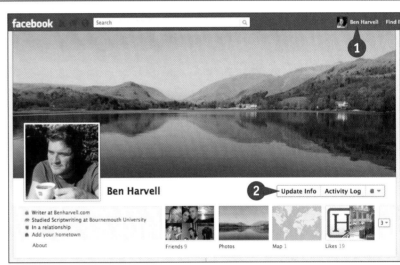

The Update info screen appears.

3 Click **Edit** next to Contact Info.

4 Click the **Other Phones** arrow (⊡) and select **Work or Home** from the pop-up menu and then type your phone number.

5 Select your country from the pop-up menu (⊡).

Ⓐ To add another phone number, click **Add another phone**.

6 Type your address information in the relevant fields.

7 Click **Save**.

Add Instant Messaging and Website Information

To show Facebook friends your website and instant messaging details, you can add them to your profile. These details appear in the Info section of your profile. The IM Screen Names section enables you to enter multiple accounts and select from a wide range of instant messaging services. This allows Facebook friends the opportunity to add you as a contact via IM clients such as Yahoo! Messenger and GoogleChat. The Website section enables you to enter the address of your own website or multiple websites. Websites appear as links on your profile page.

Add Instant Messaging and Website Information

1 Click your name at the top right of the screen.

2 Click **Update Info**.

The Update Info window opens.

3 Click **Edit** next to Contact Info.

4 Click the **IM Screen Names** arrow (⬦) and select an instant messaging account from the pop-up menu.

5 Type your instant messaging screen name.

Ⓐ To add another screen name, click the **Add another screen name** link.

6 Type your website address here.

7 Click **Save**.

Note: You may enter multiple website addresses.

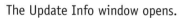

Set a Facebook Username

By claiming a Facebook username, your account becomes easier to find and share and is personalized with a unique web address. Instead of the basic Facebook URL, you can pick a unique username that appears after the facebook.com/ portion of the website in your browser's URL bar. This could be your own name or a memorable word. You can choose your username and check its availability before applying it, but you can change your username only once.

Set a Facebook Username

1 Type **www.facebook.com/ username** into your browser's URL bar.

Ⓐ If you want to use one of the suggested usernames, select an option (□ changes ◉).

2 Click **More** to expand the dialog box.

3 Type the username you want to use.

4 Click **Check Availability**.

A message box appears.

5 Click **Confirm**.

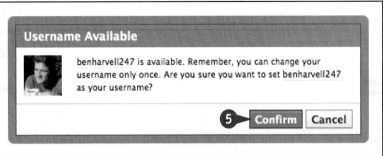

CHAPTER 2

Setting Security

Enhance the security of your Facebook account by adjusting settings
for logging in, using apps, and editing e-mail and password settings.
You can also set notifications to tell you when your account has been
accessed and allow only approved computers and devices to log in to
your Facebook account.

Set a Security Question

Setting a security question adds an additional level of safety to your Facebook account. Should you lose access to your Facebook account or forget your password, you can use the security question to help identify yourself. Select a question and answer that only you know to avoid people guessing it easily. Also, pick a memorable question and answer so you can remember it when the time comes to use it.

Set a Security Question

1 Click the **Account** menu (▾).

2 Click **Account Settings**.

3 Click **Security** from the left column.

4 Click the **Security Question** section.

The Security Question section expands.

5 Click the **Question** arrow (▾) and select a question from the pop-up menu.

6 Type your answer.

7 Type your password.

8 Click **Save Changes**.

Using Secure Browsing

Turning on the Secure Browsing feature for your Facebook account turns on HTTPS encryption while you use your account. This encryption makes it more difficult for people to access your information without permission, and is definitely worth turning on if you regularly use your Facebook account on computers you do not own. Once turned on, HTTPS Secure Browsing remains active until turned off, but Facebook Mobile does not currently support it.

Using Secure Browsing

1 Click the **Account** menu (⊡).

2 Click **Account Settings**.

3 Click **Security** from the left column.

4 Click **Edit** in the Secure Browsing section.

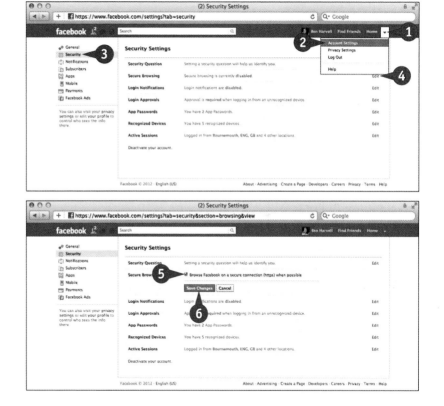

The Secure Browsing section expands.

5 Click the **Secure Browsing** box (☐ changes to ☑).

6 Click **Save Changes**.

Set Login Notifications

Login Notifications let you know when your Facebook account is accessed from a computer or mobile device you have not used before. These notifications can help to alert you to a potential security violation, especially if you use only one computer or mobile device to access your account. You should also turn this option on if you have used your account on a shared computer. Notifications can be sent via e-mail or as a text message or push notification to your mobile phone.

Set Login Notifications

1. Click the **Account** menu (▾).

2. Click **Account Settings**.

3. Click **Security** from the left column.

4. Click **Edit** in the Login Notifications section.

The Login Notifications section expands.

5. Click the **Email** box (☐ changes to ☑) to receive notifications via e-mail.

6. Click the **Text message/Push notification** box (☐ changes to ☑) to receive notifications via text or push notification.

7. Click **Save Changes**.

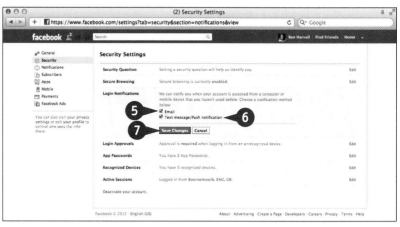

Set Login Approval

Login approvals make it harder for unauthorized people to access your account on a computer or device that you have not used with Facebook before. When you attempt to log in to Facebook on an unrecognized computer or device, Facebook sends a security code to your mobile phone that needs to be entered before granting access. A mobile phone must be registered with your Facebook account to use this feature, and that mobile phone must be present during the Login Approval setup process.

Set Login Approval

① Click the **Account** menu (▾).

② Click **Account Settings**.

③ Click **Security** from the left column.

④ Click **Edit** in the Login Approvals section.

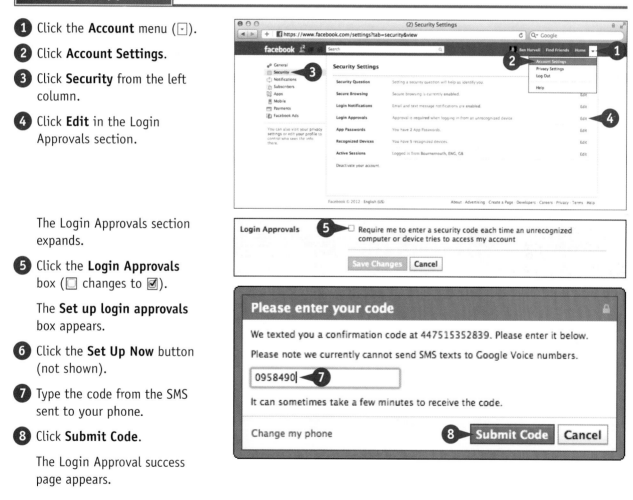

The Login Approvals section expands.

⑤ Click the **Login Approvals** box (☐ changes to ☑).

The **Set up login approvals** box appears.

⑥ Click the **Set Up Now** button (not shown).

⑦ Type the code from the SMS sent to your phone.

⑧ Click **Submit Code**.

The Login Approval success page appears.

Set App Passwords

Rather than using your Facebook password with apps that access your Facebook account, you can opt to use App Passwords. If you are using Login Approvals to send you a message each time you log in from a new computer, you must use a code each time you access an app. These one-time passwords make it possible to access apps without having to wait for a code because the apps have been assigned their own password from the App Passwords settings screen.

Set App Passwords

1 Click the **Account** menu (⏷).

2 Click **Account Settings**.

3 Click **Security** from the left column.

4 Click **Edit** in the App Passwords section.

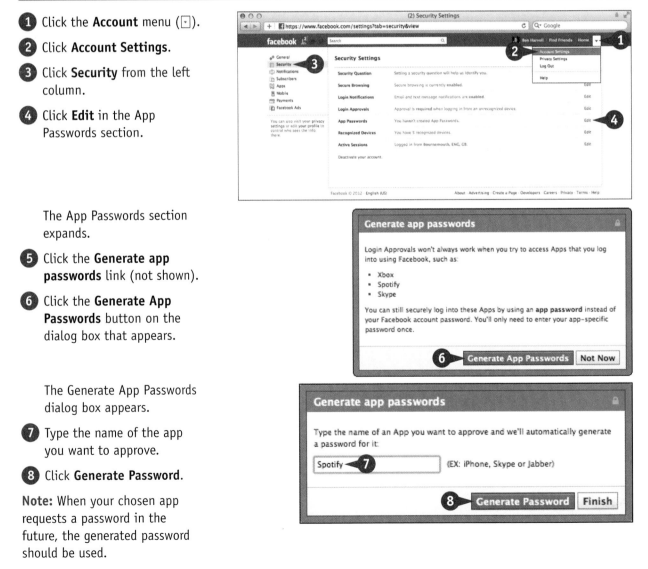

The App Passwords section expands.

5 Click the **Generate app passwords** link (not shown).

6 Click the **Generate App Passwords** button on the dialog box that appears.

The Generate App Passwords dialog box appears.

7 Type the name of the app you want to approve.

8 Click **Generate Password**.

Note: When your chosen app requests a password in the future, the generated password should be used.

Edit and View Recognized Devices

The Recognized Devices section of Facebook's Security Settings screen shows any devices that have been authorized to use your Facebook account. Devices appear here only if you are already using Login Approvals. Each time you log in to Facebook from an unknown device and use a code sent to your phone to authorize the device, the device is added to this list. You can remove a device, when you update or lose it, by visiting the Recognized Devices section and selecting which device to remove.

Edit and View Recognized Devices

1 Click the **Account** menu (⊡).

2 Click **Account Settings**.

3 Click **Security** from the left column.

4 Click **Edit** in the Recognized Devices section.

The Recognized Devices section expands.

A All recognized devices are listed using the name you gave them and the date they were registered.

B To remove a recognized device, click **Remove**.

5 Click **Save Changes**.

View Your Active Sessions

The Active Sessions area within Security Settings shows where and when your Facebook account has been accessed recently. Most of the time this just shows when you have logged in to your account, but if you are worried someone else may be accessing your account, it is a useful place to check. From this screen you can also end an active session that you do not recognize to prevent further access to your account. The locations included in Active Sessions are only approximate, and this feature does not currently work with mobile Facebook.

View Your Active Sessions

1 Click the **Account** menu ([▾]).

2 Click **Account Settings**.

3 Click **Security** from the left column.

4 Click **Edit** in the Active Sessions section.

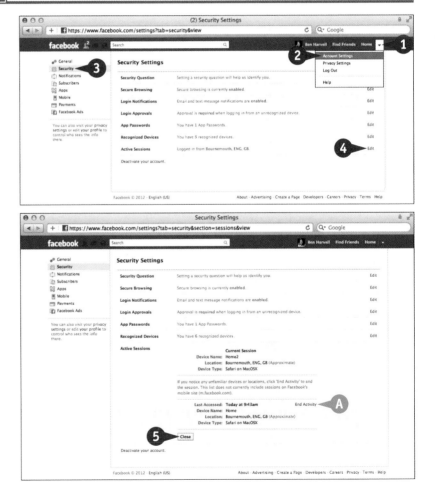

The Active Sessions section expands showing your recent sessions, locations, and devices.

Ⓐ If you see any locations for which you have not logged into Facebook, click **End Activity**.

5 Click **Close**.

Change Your Primary E-Mail

If you list more than one e-mail address on your Facebook account settings, you can set which e-mail account Facebook should use by default. The primary e-mail account is where Facebook notifications are sent, and is also used for security purposes such as resetting your password or regaining access to your account. Only one e-mail address can be used as a primary e-mail, and you must have access to that account at all times, so using your primary home e-mail account is usually best. It is even better if your e-mail account is web-based, like iCloud or Gmail account for example, so you can access your account from any computer connected to the Internet.

Change Your Primary E-Mail

1 Click the **Account** menu (⊡).

2 Click **Account Settings**.

3 Click **Edit** in the Email section.

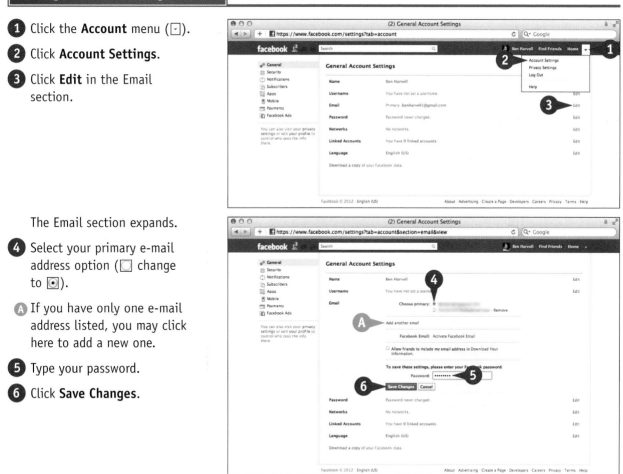

The Email section expands.

4 Select your primary e-mail address option (☐ change to ◉).

Ⓐ If you have only one e-mail address listed, you may click here to add a new one.

5 Type your password.

6 Click **Save Changes**.

Change Your Password

Your Facebook password is one of the most important pieces of information relating to your account. You can change your password at any time by visiting the Account Settings page. Making sure that your password is not only memorable but also difficult for anyone to guess is very important. Try using a combination of numbers and letters as a way to make your password harder to crack or guess.

Change Your Password

1 Click the **Account** menu (□).

2 Click **Account Settings**.

3 Click **Edit** in the Password section.

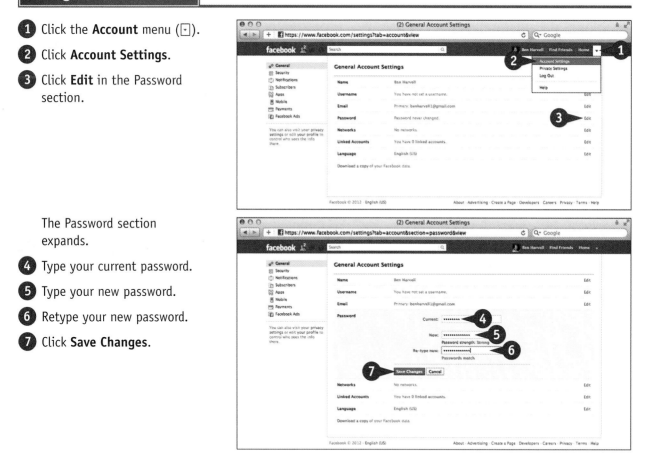

The Password section expands.

4 Type your current password.

5 Type your new password.

6 Retype your new password.

7 Click **Save Changes**.

Set Your Language

By default Facebook uses U.S. English for page titles, explanations, and any other text within your account aside from content added by friends. You can change the default language used on your Facebook account at any time from the Account Settings screen. You can choose from a wide range of commonly used languages as well as some novelty options including Pirate and Upside Down. Once saved, the language you choose is applied across your entire Facebook account.

Set Your Language

1 Click the **Account** menu ([·]).

2 Click **Account Settings**.

3 Click **Edit** in the Language section.

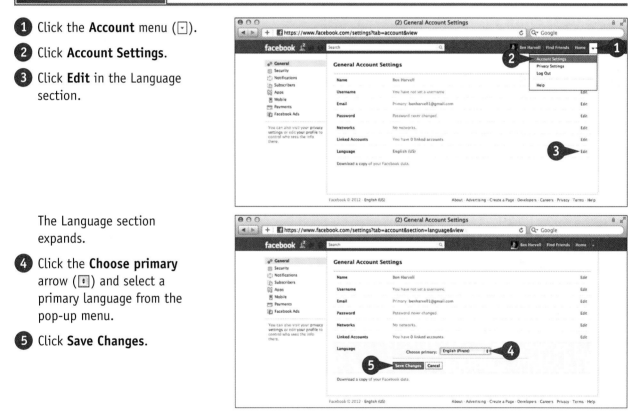

The Language section expands.

4 Click the **Choose primary** arrow ([·]) and select a primary language from the pop-up menu.

5 Click **Save Changes**.

Link Your Accounts

A linked account is an account that another service provides that can be tied to your Facebook account so you do not need to log in to both at the same time. For example, if you link a Google account to your Facebook account, you will not have to log in to Facebook to share links from Google to Facebook, or click the Facebook Like button on a website when visited through your Google account. Linked accounts can be added or removed by visiting the Linked Accounts section under Account Settings.

Link Your Accounts

1 Click the **Account** menu (⊡).

2 Click **Account Settings**.

3 Click **Edit** in the Linked Accounts section.

The Linked Accounts section expands.

4 Click the **Linked Accounts** arrow (⊡) and select an account from the pop-up menu.

5 Click **Link New Account**.

The Link New Account dialog box appears.

6 Type your Facebook password.

7 Click **Confirm**.

8 Click **Continue**.

If you are not already logged in, a new browser window opens with a login interface for your account.

9 Type your e-mail address.

10 Type your password.

11 Click **Sign in**.

Your linked account is now added.

How do I remove a linked account?
Visit the General Account Settings screen and click **Edit** next to Linked Accounts. Locate the linked account you want to remove and click **Remove** next to it. The linked account is removed and you must log in to that account and to Facebook to send information from one to the other. You can return to this screen at any time and link the account again or choose a new account to link to your Facebook account.

Download Your Facebook Data

You can download all the data associated with your Facebook account to your computer at any time. All information from your profile, posts, and comments on your timeline, notes, events, and messages are downloaded. All your photos and videos as well as a list of your friends are also included in the download. This option can help you to create a backup of your account and also offers a simple way to access all your photos for organizing on your computer.

Download Your Facebook Data

1 Click the **Account** menu ([▾]).

2 Click **Account Settings**.

3 Click the **Download a copy of your Facebook data** link.

The Download Your Information screen appears.

4 Click **Start My Archive**.

The Request My Download box appears.

5 Click **Start My Archive**.

An e-mail will be sent to you with a download link when your archive is ready to download.

Deactivate Your Account

I f you want to leave Facebook and shut down your account, you can do so from the Account
Settings screen. When you deactivate your account, your profile disappears from Facebook and
nobody can search for you or information about you. You can always reactivate your account after
deactivation if you want to by logging in to your Facebook account. Until you do, however, your
account is closed and your profile is invisible.

Deactivate Your Account

1 Click the **Account** menu (□).

2 Click **Account Settings**.

3 Click **Security** from the left
column.

4 Click the **Deactivate your
account** link.

The Deactivate Account
screen opens.

5 Select a reason for leaving
(□ changes to ☑).

6 Type your reason for leaving.

7 To opt out of receiving future
e-mail from Facebook, click
this box (□ changes to ☑).

8 Click **Confirm**.

CHAPTER 3

Setting Privacy

Facebook privacy settings let you control who can see information about you and the photos, videos, and other updates you post. You can also set how you connect with friends on Facebook and determine how much of your information is shared with apps, games, and websites via Facebook.

Use the Audience Selector to Control Privacy

The Audience Selector controls who can see a specific status update, photo, video, or any other information you add to Facebook. Each time you add new information to Facebook, you can set the privacy level for it, whether you want everyone to see it, only your friends, or specific lists of people. The Audience Selector appears next to the Post button when you update your status, add a photo, or check in to a location. You can also set a default privacy setting in order to always show or hide content from set groups when you post to Facebook, unless you set the Audience Selector menu to a different setting.

Use the Audience Selector to Control Privacy

1 Click **Update Status**.

2 Click the **Audience Selector** menu ( ).

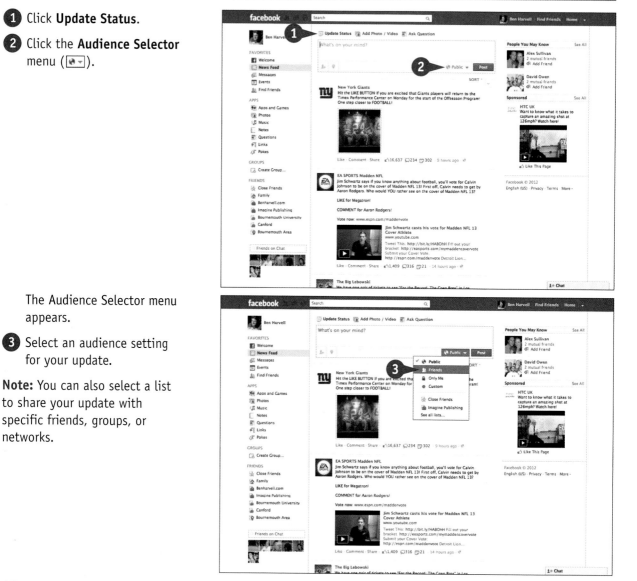

The Audience Selector menu appears.

3 Select an audience setting for your update.

Note: You can also select a list to share your update with specific friends, groups, or networks.

Create a Custom Privacy Setting

The Facebook Audience Selector offers a custom privacy setting through which you can create your own specific privacy setting for posts. The custom option appears on the Audience Selector menu and launches a new Custom Privacy box within which you can fine-tune your privacy settings and select friends from whom to hide your update. There are a number of reasons to use the Custom Privacy setting, such as planning a surprise for a friend or excluding work colleagues from conversations you may have outside of work.

Create a Custom Privacy Setting

1 Click **Update Status.**

2 Click the **Audience Selector** menu (📷▾) and select **Custom.**

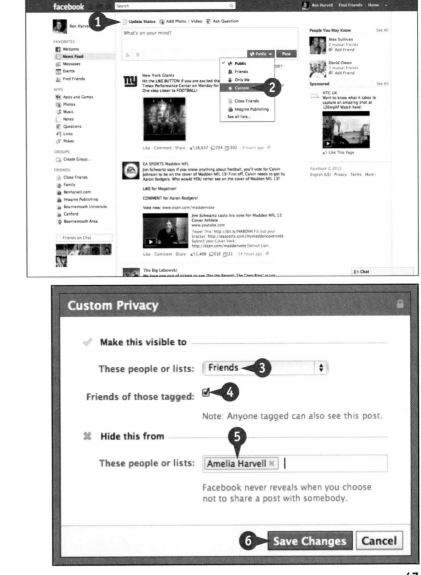

The Custom Privacy box appears.

3 Click the arrow (▾) and select a group from the pop-up menu.

4 Check the **Friends of those tagged** option to see your update (☐ changes to ☑).

5 Type friends' names or friend lists to hide the update from them.

6 Click **Save Changes.**

Set Default Privacy Levels

Facebook allows for a default privacy level to be set so that you do not have to use the Audience Selector each time you post to Facebook. Setting a default privacy level helps you to retain your required privacy settings when you are using Facebook on a platform that does not offer the Audience Selector, such as the Facebook app for mobile devices. Setting the default privacy level to private or friends can also help prevent posting content publicly by accident if you do not remember to use the Audience Selector when posting.

Set Default Privacy Levels

1 Click the **Account** menu.

2 Click **Privacy Settings**.

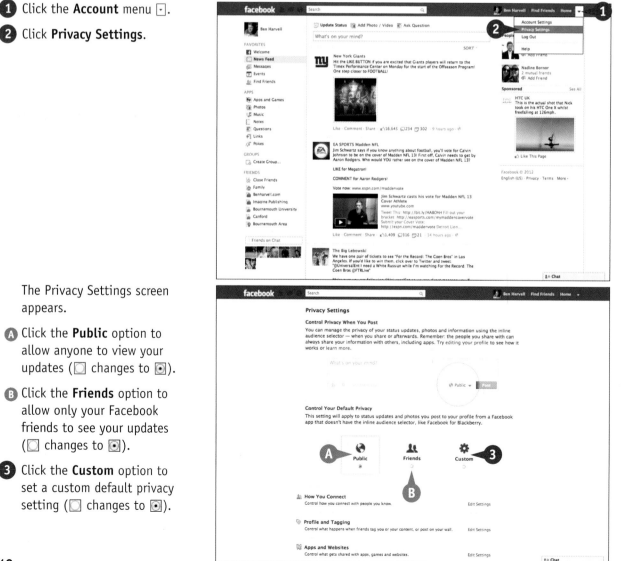

The Privacy Settings screen appears.

A Click the **Public** option to allow anyone to view your updates (☐ changes to ◉).

B Click the **Friends** option to allow only your Facebook friends to see your updates (☐ changes to ◉).

3 Click the **Custom** option to set a custom default privacy setting (☐ changes to ◉).

The Custom Privacy dialog box appears.

④ Click the arrow (⬚) and select a group to share your updates with from the pop-up menu.

Ⓒ To allow friends of those tagged to see your updates, click the **Friends of those tagged** option (☐ becomes ☑).

⑤ Type the names of friends or a list name to hide updates from them.

⑥ Click **Save Changes**.

Ⓓ The Friend Selector now shows Custom.

Custom Privacy

✓ Make this visible to
These people or lists: Friends ◀④ ⬚

Friends of those tagged: ☑◀Ⓒ
Note: Anyone tagged can also see this post.

✗ Hide this from
These people or lists: Jonathan Cockerton ✗ |
Facebook never reveals when you choose not to share a post with somebody.

⑥ Save Changes Cancel

facebook Search Ben Harvell Find Friends Home

Privacy Settings

Control Privacy When You Post
You can manage the privacy of your status updates, photos and information using the inline audience selector — when you share or afterwards. Remember: the people you share with can always share your information with others, including apps. Try editing your profile to see how it works or learn more.

What's on your mind?

Ⓓ Custom ▾ Post

Control Your Default Privacy
This setting will apply to status updates and photos you post to your profile from a Facebook app that doesn't have the inline audience selector, like Facebook for Blackberry.

🌐 Public   👥 Friends   ⚙ Custom

How You Connect
Control how you connect with people you know. Edit Settings

Profile and Tagging
Control what happens when friends tag you or your content, or post on your wall. Edit Settings

Apps and Websites
Control what gets shared with apps, games and websites. Edit Settings   Chat

What does the Friends of Those Tagged check box do?
When checked, this option allows friends of anyone tagged in your status update, photo, or video section to view your posting. Friends of those tagged in your update section do not have to be your friends to see your post when this box is checked under the custom privacy settings.

Why can I not access the Audience Selector when using Mobile Facebook?
Certain platforms do not offer the Audience Selector option when you post to Facebook. This includes Facebook for Blackberry. In this case, Facebook uses the default privacy setting you have chosen.

Control Your Profile's Appearance in Search Engines

By default, a preview of your Facebook profile shows up when somebody searches for your name with a search engine like Google. To prevent this from happening, you can turn off the public search feature within Facebook. Having a profile preview appear in search results can be useful to help people find and add you as a friend on Facebook, but if you want to keep your profile completely private, you should disable the public search feature.

Control Your Profile's Appearance in Search Engines

① Click the **Account** menu ⊡.

② Click **Privacy Settings.**

③ Click **Edit Settings** in the Apps and Websites section.

④ Click **Edit Settings** in the Public search section.

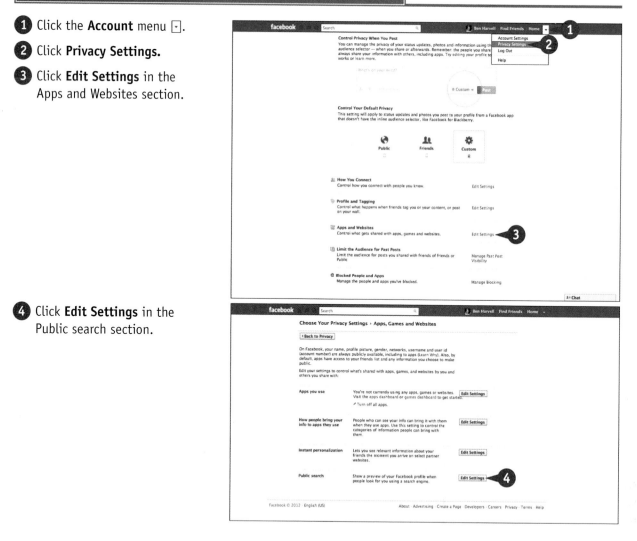

The Public Search Privacy
Settings screen appears.

5 Uncheck **Enable public
search** (☑changes to ☐).

Choose Your Privacy Settings ▸ Public Search

◂ Back to Apps

Public search   Public search controls whether people who enter your name in a search engine will see a
                    preview of your Facebook profile. Because some search engines cache information, some
                    of your profile information may be available for a period of time after you turn public
                    search off. See preview

                    ☑ Enable public search

The Are You Sure? dialog
box appears.

6 Click **Confirm.**

Are you sure?

When real world friends look for you using a search engine, this
setting makes it possible for them to see a preview of your
Facebook profile (containing only info that's public). If you
continue, friends may not know if it's really you.

6 ▸ Confirm   Cancel

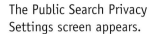

**What information can people see if I
have public search enabled?**

A preview of your Facebook timeline,
including your profile picture and any
other information that you have set as
public, is visible when somebody clicks
on your profile in search engine results.

**I disabled public search but my profile still appears in
search engine results.**

Because of the way some search engines collect and cache
information, it may take a while for your Facebook profile
preview to stop showing up in search results. Keep the
public search feature disabled and check search results
regularly and your profile will soon disappear from searches.

Control How You Connect with Others

You can set who can contact you via Facebook and access your contact information via Facebook's Privacy Settings screen. Using these settings you can limit the number of people who can see your e-mail address, phone number, and instant messenger usernames, and also who can send you friend requests or messages on Facebook. By default, these settings are configured to allow everyone to access your information and get in touch with you, but you can quickly block specific people or groups from accessing your contact details or adding you as a friend.

Control How You Connect with Others

1 Click the **Account** menu (⏷).

2 Click **Privacy Settings**.

3 Click **Edit Settings** in the How You Connect section.

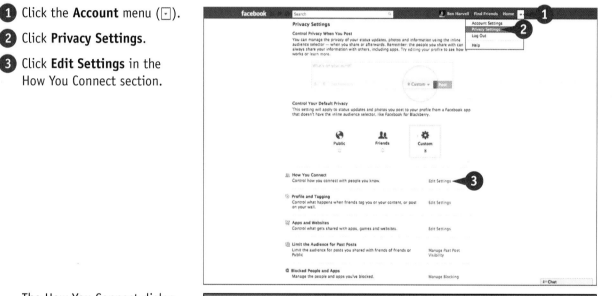

The How You Connect dialog box appears.

4 Click the **Audience Selector** (⏷) and select **Everyone** next to each setting that you want to edit.

5 Select a group option from the menu.

6 Click **Done**.

Set Who Can See and Post on Your Timeline

Your Facebook timeline is the central point for all the information and media you post, as well as a place where friends can comment on your posts. Facebook's privacy settings enable you to set who can post to your timeline, and who can see what others post on your timeline. You can also set who can see posts on your timeline in which you have been tagged. This additional privacy feature helps you to control how your timeline appears to others and to manage the comments made on it.

Set Who Can See and Post on Your Timeline

1 Click the **Account** menu ().

2 Click **Privacy Settings**.

3 Click **Edit Settings** in the Profile and Tagging section.

4 Click the **Audience Selector** menu () and select who can post on your timeline.

5 Click the **Audience Selector** menu () and select who can see items posted on your timeline.

6 Click the **Audience Selector** menu () and select who can see posts in which you have been tagged on your timeline.

7 Click **Done**.

Turn On Profile Review

You can set your Facebook privacy settings to allow you to review when you are tagged in posts by others. With Profile Review turned off, any of your friends can tag you in a post which will then appear on your profile. When it is turned on, you must approve a tag before it is added to a post. If somebody you are not friends with on Facebook adds a tag to one of your posts, you are always asked to review it regardless of whether Profile Review is enabled or disabled.

Turn On Profile Review

1 Click the **Account** menu ([-]).

2 Click **Privacy Settings**.

3 Click **Edit Settings** in the Profile and Tagging section.

The Profile and Tagging dialog box appears.

4 Click **Off**.

5 Click **Disabled**.

6 Click **Enabled** from the menu.

7 Click **Back**.

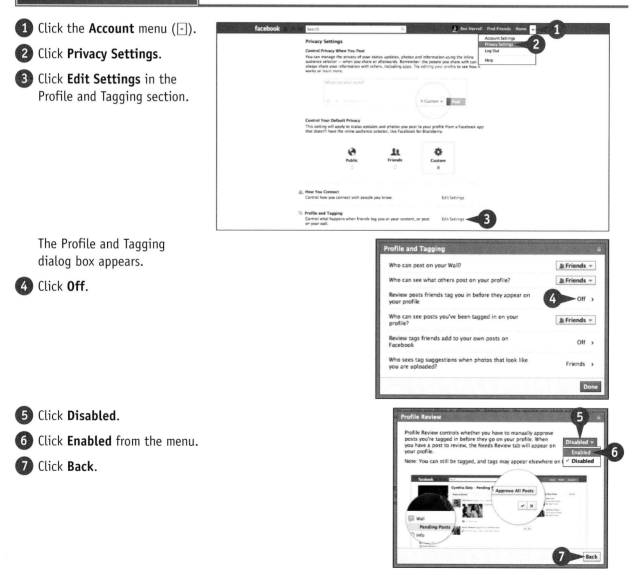

Turn Off Tag Suggestions for Photos

When one of your friends uploads a photo to Facebook, Facebook may recognize the image as you, using face recognition, and suggest your friend tags you in the photograph. Within Facebook's privacy settings, you can allow Tag Suggestions to be made or you can turn them off, so friends are never shown your name in a list of tag suggestions they may receive when uploading a photo. There are two settings for Tag Suggestions, Friends and No One. By default, Tag Suggestions is set to Friends and tag suggestions will therefore be made to friends uploading photos of you or someone who Facebook thinks is you.

Turn Off Tag Suggestions

1 Click the **Account** menu (⏷).

2 Click **Privacy Settings**.

3 Click **Edit Settings** in the Profile and Tagging section.

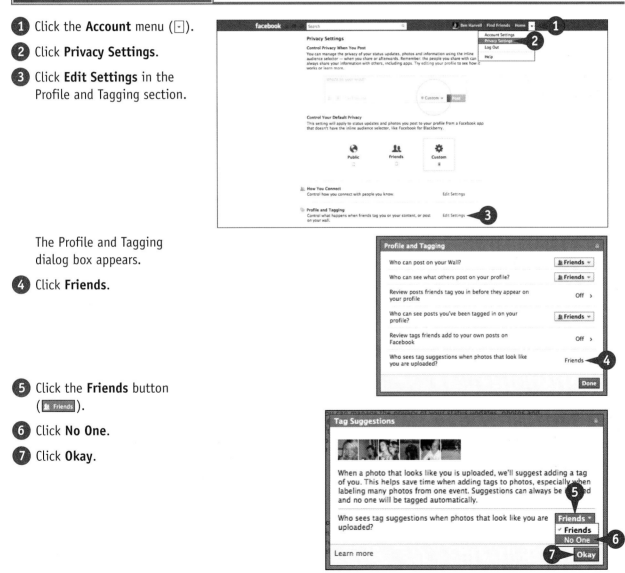

The Profile and Tagging dialog box appears.

4 Click **Friends**.

5 Click the **Friends** button (Friends).

6 Click **No One**.

7 Click **Okay**.

Set Access Levels for Facebook Apps

Hundreds of Facebook apps are available that require different pieces of information from your account in order to work. Apps you install on Facebook could be games, connections to websites, and desktop software, or other social networks and online services. Using the App Settings screen, you can determine which information from your account an app can access via Facebook and who can see posts made by apps you have installed.

Set Access Levels for Facebook Apps

1 Click the **Account** menu (□).

2 Click **Privacy Settings**.

3 Click **Edit Settings** in the Apps and Websites section.

The Apps, Games, and Websites privacy settings appear.

4 Click the **Edit Settings** button for Apps you use.

The App Settings window appears.

5 Select an app.

6 Click the **Edit** link next to it.

The app's information appears.

A Click **Remove app** to uninstall it.

B This section shows what functions the app is allowed to perform.

C Click the X to prevent an app from performing a function.

D This section shows when the app last accessed your Facebook data.

7 Click the **Audience Selector** menu ( ) and select who can see posts from this app.

8 Click the **Notifications** arrow ( ) and select when you want the app to send a notification.

9 Click **Close**.

App Settings

You have authorized these apps to interact with your Facebook account:

Words With Friends   Less than 24 hours ago   Edit ×

Angry Birds ◀ **5**   Less than 24 hours ago   **6** ▶ Edit ×

App Settings

You have authorized these apps to interact with your Facebook account:

Words With Friends   Less than 24 hours ago   Edit ×

Angry Birds   Last logged in: Less than 24 hours ago   Remove app ◀ **A**

This app needs: • Your e-mail address (benharvell1@gmail.com)

B ▶ This app can also: ▦ Post on my behalf   × ◀ **C**

Last data access: **D** ▶ No data access recorded
                             Learn more

Posts on my behalf: Who can see posts this app makes for me on my   **7** ▶ ⚙ Custom ▾
                            Facebook timeline?

Notifications: When to notify me?   **8** ▶ The app sends me a req... ▾

                    9 ▶ Close

TIPS

I have no apps listed in my App Settings screen. Where are they?

If you have not installed any apps or have removed any apps you had installed, this page appears blank. Apps can be installed from the Facebook Apps page or when recommended to you by friends. When you have installed Facebook apps, you can edit the their settings from the App Settings screen.

Why would an app post on my behalf?

Certain apps, like games or online services, send posts to your timeline to tell your friends about your activity. This could include watching a movie, listening to music, or playing a game, among other pieces of information.

Block Facebook Users

Using someone's name or e-mail address, you can block a user from ever contacting you on Facebook. Once a person is blocked, they cannot interact with you on Facebook and cannot send friend requests or view any of your posts. You can also unblock users at any time by heading back to the Manage Blocking section of the Facebook Privacy Settings screen. This feature can be useful to prevent spam requests on Facebook or avoid being pestered by unwanted invites.

Block Facebook Users

1 Click the **Account** menu (⊡).

2 Click **Privacy Settings**.

3 Click **Manage Blocking**.

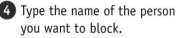

Block a Person by Name

The Manage Blocking window appears.

4 Type the name of the person you want to block.

5 Click **Block**.

The Block People window appears.

6 Click **Block** next to the person you want to block.

7 Click **Close**.

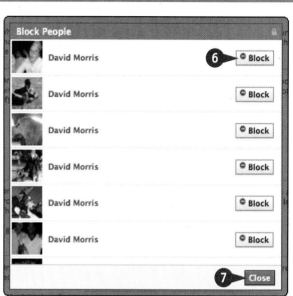

Block an E-Mail Address

8 Type the e-mail address of the person you want to block.

9 Click **Block**.

10 Repeat steps **6** and **7**.

How do I unblock someone?
People you have blocked appear in the Block Users section beneath the Name and Email fields. Click **Unblock** next to a person's name to unblock him or her, or click **Remove** next to an e-mail address to remove that e-mail account from your block list.

Are people notified when they are blocked?
Facebook does not notify users when another user blocks them. Blocked users will be unable to friend you on Facebook or interact with you on Facebook unless you both use a particular app, game, or are members of a group. In these cases, you may see posts or other activity from that person.

Limit the Audience for Past Posts

If you are not sure whether a post was made public or just to friends, or you have made posts without choosing an audience, you can set all your past posts to be visible only to friends. Although you can change the privacy level of individual posts, this process offers a bulk method to ensure that any post you have ever made on Facebook is visible only to your friends.

Limit the Audience for Past Posts

1 Click the **Account** menu (⊡).

2 Click **Privacy Settings**.

3 Click **Manage Past Post Visibility**.

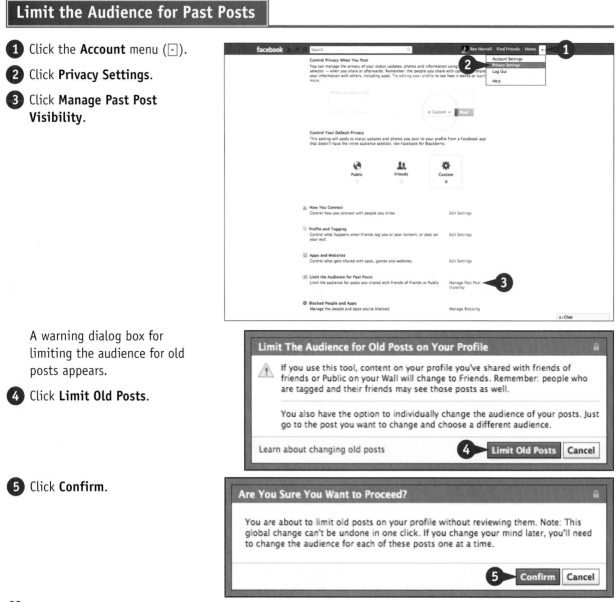

A warning dialog box for limiting the audience for old posts appears.

4 Click **Limit Old Posts**.

5 Click **Confirm**.

See What Your Timeline Looks Like to Other People

You can check your privacy settings at any time by using the View As feature. This setting shows how your timeline looks to the public or Facebook users who are not your friends. You can also type a friend's name to see exactly what he or she sees when viewing your profile. Viewing your profile in this way can be useful for spotting posts without the correct privacy setting. You can then adjust the setting with the Audience Selector to rectify the situation.

See What Your Timeline Looks Like to Other People

1 Click your name at the top right of the interface.

2 Click the **Settings** button (⚙).

3 Click **View As....**

Your profile appears as shown to the public.

Ⓐ You can type a friend's name and press Enter (Return) to see how your profile looks to him or her.

Ⓑ You can click other sections of your account to see how they look to others.

4 Click **Back to Timeline.**

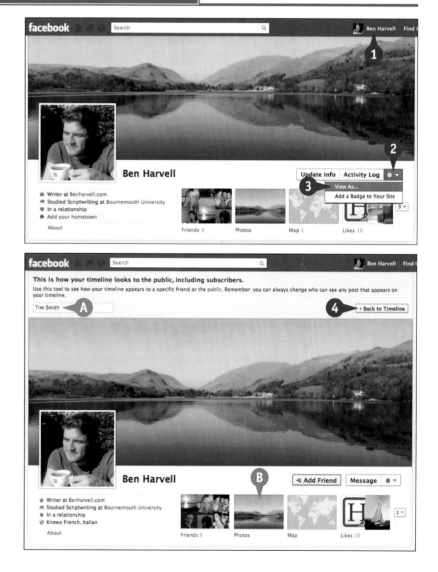

CHAPTER 4

Finding and Organizing Friends

To make the most of Facebook, you need to find and add friends by importing contacts from your e-mail accounts, or by simply searching on Facebook. You can also find people to add as friends on Facebook by viewing suggestions.

Find Friends by Importing Contacts

Finding friends on Facebook is easy and gets easier the more friends you add. As Facebook begins to understand your friend networks and groups, it suggests friends that it thinks you might know. In order to achieve this, you need to add as many of your existing friends as possible. This can be done by giving Facebook access to your existing communication services, such as e-mail accounts or IM services. You can use multiple accounts to find your friends by clicking **Find Friends** again and selecting another e-mail account or service from the list.

Find Friends by Importing Contacts

1 Click **Find Friends**.

Note: If **Find Friends** is not listed in the left column, search for Find Friends in the Search box at the top of the screen and click the first result.

2 Select an account and click **Find Friends**.

3 Type your username and password.

Note: Different services may ask for different login information.

4 Click **Find Friends**.

Note: A login window may appear asking you to enter your password again.

A list of contacts already using Facebook is shown.

5 Select the friends you want to add (☐ changes to ☑).

6 Click **Add Friends**.

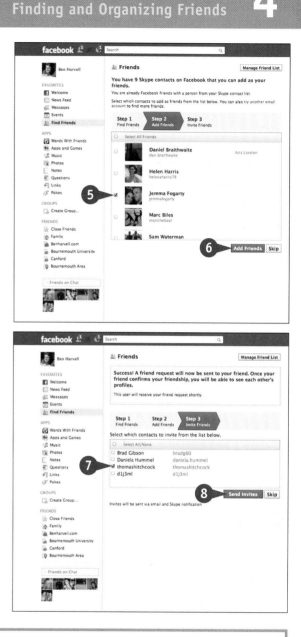

Friend requests are sent to all the friends you selected, and a list of additional contacts appears.

7 Select friends not on Facebook to invite by e-mail (☐ changes to ☑).

8 Click **Send Invites**.

What happens when I invite a friend by e-mail?
Facebook sends an e-mail to the e-mail address of the person you selected. The e-mail explains that you have joined Facebook and want them to create an account and become friends. The e-mail also includes a link so that your friend can quickly visit the Facebook sign-up page.

Does Facebook store my account details when I search for friends?
No. Facebook only uses your login details to search for contacts and does not store your password. If you want to use the same account on Facebook in the future, you will be asked to enter your password again.

Accept and Ignore Friend Requests

When somebody requests to become friends with you on Facebook, you have the option to ignore or accept the request. Friend request notifications are shown at the top of the Facebook interface, and you can view a list of friend requests at any time by clicking the **Friend Requests** button. If you accept a friend request you are instantly linked to the person who requested, you become friends, and he or she is notified. If you ignore a friend request, no notification is sent to the other user.

Accept and Ignore Friend Requests

1 Click the **Friend Requests** button ( ).

2 Click **See All Friend Requests**.

Ⓐ You can also click **Confirm** or **Not Now** on this menu to accept or ignore a friend request.

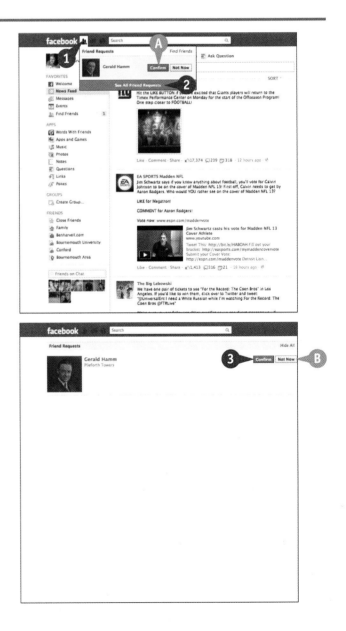

The Confirm Requests screen appears.

3 Select the friend's request that you would like to accept and click **Confirm**.

Ⓑ To ignore a request, click **Not Now**.

Note: If you have previously clicked **Not Now** for a friend request, you can view these requests again by clicking the **See Hidden Requests** link that appears on this page.

View Your Friends

You can view a list of all your current Facebook friends at any time by clicking the **Friends** link on the left of the Facebook interface or, if you are using the Facebook Timeline, by clicking the **Friends** link below your timeline cover image. This screen shows the profile picture and name of each of your friends and allows you to quickly access a friend's profile page by clicking his or her name or image.

View Your Friends

1 Click your name at the top right of the interface.

2 Click **Friends**.

Note: If you are using Facebook Timeline, the **Friends** link appears below your timeline cover picture.

All your current friends are shown.

A You can use the search bar to type a friend's name.

3 Position your mouse pointer over a friend's name to view his or her basic profile information.

4 Click a friend's name or picture to view his or her profile.

Unfriend People on Facebook

I f you want to end a Facebook friendship, you can select the **Unfriend** option from the Friends menu wherever a friend is mentioned on Facebook. This can be on your news feed, timeline, or within your friend list or Messages screen. When you unfriend people on Facebook, they stop seeing your posts and you stop seeing theirs. No notification is sent to those you have unfriended; they simply stop seeing your posts and lose access to viewing your profile information.

Unfriend People on Facebook

Remove a Friend via Profile Page

1 Click your name at the top right of the interface.

2 Click **Friends** from the left column or beneath your timeline image.

3 Click a friend's name or picture.

Your friend's timeline page appears.

4 Position your mouse pointer over the **Friends** button to view the menu.

5 Click **Unfriend**.

The Remove as a Friend?
dialog box appears.

6 Click **Remove from Friends**.

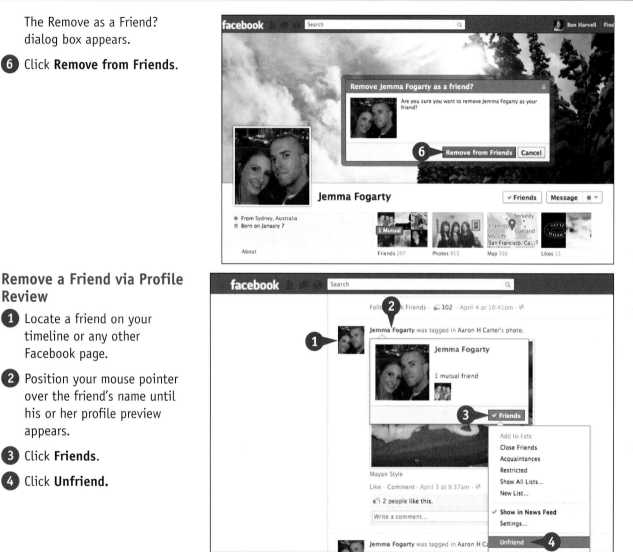

Remove a Friend via Profile Review

1 Locate a friend on your timeline or any other Facebook page.

2 Position your mouse pointer over the friend's name until his or her profile preview appears.

3 Click **Friends**.

4 Click **Unfriend.**

I made a mistake. How do I undo my unfriend?
There is no way to take back an unfriending. You have to send a friend request to the person you unfriended and they must accept it before you can be friends on Facebook again.

What is the difference between unfriending and blocking?
Unfriending simply ends your friendship and interaction with another person on Facebook. You can become friends again at any time. When a person is blocked they cannot send a friend request or communicate with the user that has blocked them.

Poke Friends

If you have not heard from some of your Facebook friends for a while or are waiting for them to respond to a message, you can poke them. Pokes are small notifications that appear on your friends' Notifications menu. They are also alerted via e-mail and text if they have those settings activated. Pokes can be used as a reminder that you have not spoken recently or to initiate a conversation on Facebook.

Poke Friends

1 Click a friend's name or picture.

Your friend's profile appears.

2 Click the **Action** menu ().

3 Click **Poke**.

Your Poke is sent to your friend.

View Your Friendship with Others

To view how you are linked to a Facebook friend as well as communication between you and photos you are both in, you can use the See Friendship feature. The feature is available from the Action menu on a friend's profile and displays your mutual friends, mutual likes, and events you have both attended. From the See Friendship page you can also look at the relationship between other people you are friends with on Facebook.

View Your Friendship with Others

1. Click the **Action** menu (⚙)
   on a friend's profile or
   timeline.

2. Click **See Friendship** from
   the pop-up menu.

The friendship page between
you and your friend is shown.

Ⓐ A picture of you and your
friend is shown where available.

Ⓑ Recent messages between you
and your friend appear in the
middle section.

Ⓒ The Mutual Friends section
appears in the left panel.

Ⓓ Explore other friends' friendship
in the right panel.

3. Click the links in the left
   column to view different
   categories of friendship
   information.

View Suggested Friends

When you have enough information added to your profile and have added friends, Facebook can suggest friends you might want to add. On your Friends page is a link to Find Friends where you can select to view friend suggestions based on your location, where you have worked, where you studied, and friends of your existing friends. You can send a friend request to any of the suggested people by clicking the **Add Friend** button.

View Suggested Friends

1 From your Friends page, click **Find Friends**.

2 Select one or more of the categories from the left column (☐ changes to ☑).

Ⓐ Friends that fit the criteria you selected appear on the page.

3 Click **Add Friend** to send a friend request.

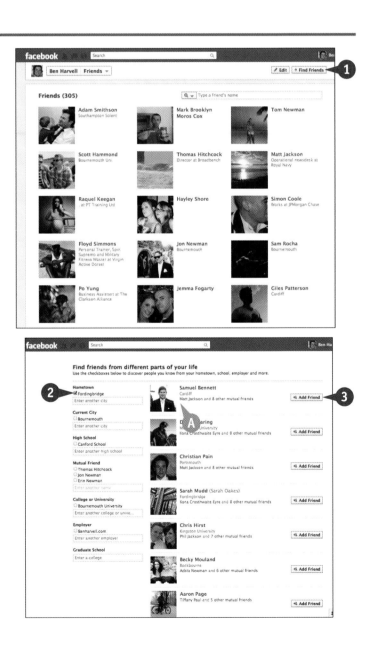

View Mutual Friends

You can view the friends you have in common with another person on Facebook by clicking the Mutual Friends link on their timeline or profile preview, as well as a number of other locations where a person's name is shown on Facebook. Clicking the Mutual Friends link shows a list of friends shared between you and somebody else on Facebook and can help to determine whether or not someone you want to add as a friend is the right person.

View Mutual Friends

1 Click the **mutual friends** link on a person's profile preview or timeline.

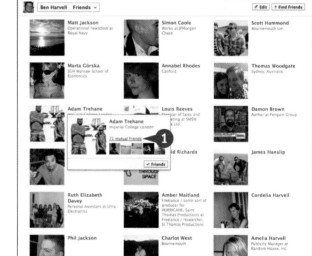

The Mutual Friends dialog box appears.

A You can change the view by clicking the **Mutual Friends** button to search friends of your friend.

2 Click **Close**.

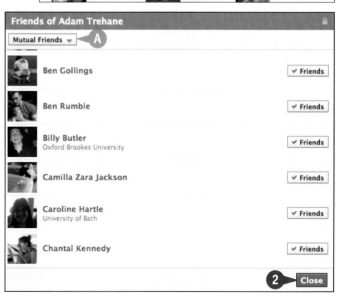

Add Friends to Lists

Friend lists are used to separate different types of friends such as close friends and acquaintances. Friends added to your Close Friends list appear more frequently in your news feed, whereas those in your Acquaintances list appear less often. There is also a Restricted list to which you can add friends you are not as close to. Friends in this list see only information you make public. You can click a list to see updates from all your friends within it and also edit the friends included in the list.

Add Friends to Lists

1. On a friend's profile, click the **Friends** button.
2. Select a list from the pop-up menu.

Your friend now appears in the list to which you added them.

Edit Work and Education Smart Lists

acebook populates smart lists automatically based on information you provided in the Education and Work and Current City information sections of your profile. Friends who listed the same school or workplace over the same time period as you are automatically added to the smart lists based on your school, university, and employers. You can edit settings for smart lists created from work and education information such as the age range of the people added to the list.

Edit Work and Education Smart Lists

1 Click **Home**.

2 Select a work or education-based smart list from the menu.

3 Click **Manage List**.

4 Click **Pick Age Range**.

The Pick an Age Range dialog box appears.

5 Click the **Age Range** arrows (⬍) and select an age range from the pop-up menu.

6 Click **Save**.

Edit Location-Based Smart Lists

Location-based smart lists use the current location information included on your profile and match it with the same information on your friends' profiles. Facebook automatically adds to the list a friend whose location is within ten miles of your current location. You can edit location-based smart list settings to make the radius smaller or larger to increase or decrease the number of friends included.

Edit Location-Based Smart Lists

1 Click **Home**.

2 Select a location-based smart list from the menu.

3 Click **Manage List**.

4 Click **Edit Radius**.

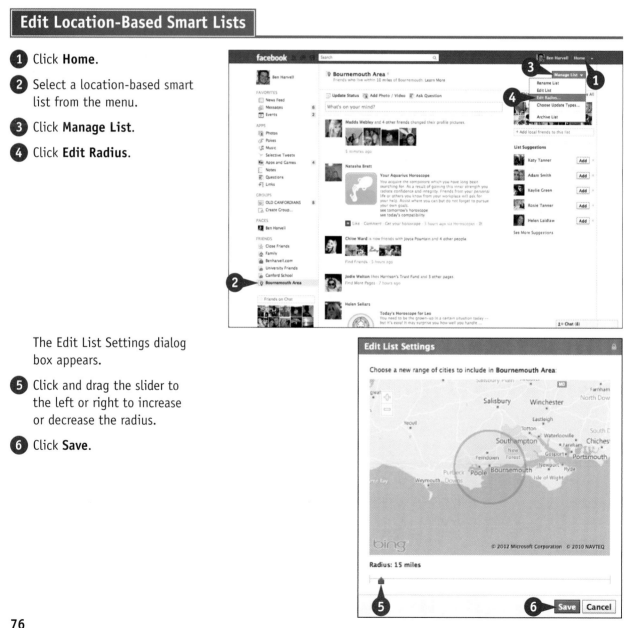

The Edit List Settings dialog box appears.

5 Click and drag the slider to the left or right to increase or decrease the radius.

6 Click **Save**.

Rename a Smart List

S mart lists can be renamed to make them unique to you and the settings you have applied to them. For example, if you change the age range of a university-based smart list to only the years you attended the university, you might want to call the smart list Classmates, instead. This can be done using the Manage List button on the smart list's page and is reflected in the left column of the Facebook interface.

Rename a Smart List

1 Click **Home**.

2 Select a smart list from the menu.

3 Click **Manage List**.

4 Click **Rename List**.

5 Type a new name for the smart list.

6 Click **Save**.

Manage and Edit Lists

As well as viewing updates from friends on your chosen list, the list view also offers the opportunity to edit the way the list works and which of your friends are included in it. Using the Manage List button, you can set what notifications you receive when friends on your list post to Facebook, and also select what type of updates are shown in your list. Using this feature can help ensure that your list only shows updates that are important to you and allows you to define the type of updates you see from friends.

Manage and Edit Lists

1. Click **Home**.

2. Select the name of the list you want to edit from the menu.

3. Click the **Notifications** button.

A. You can select whether to receive notifications from the group on Facebook, via e-mail, or not at all.

4. Click the **Manage List** button.

B. You can **Choose Update Types** to select updates you do not want to be shown in your list.

5. Click **Edit List**.

The Edit Close Friends dialog box appears.

6 Position your mouse pointer over a friend's photo and click the X to remove him or her from the list.

7 Click **Finish**.

The list page reflects your changes.

Are people notified when I add them to a list?

No. You are the only person who can view your list and see who is on the list. Similarly, people are not notified when they are removed from a list either.

What is the difference between the Close Friends and Acquaintances lists?

Updates from friends on your Close Friends list appear more often in your news feed by comparison to those on your Acquaintances list. You also have the option to hide posts from those on your Acquaintances list by using the **Audience Selector** menu ([image]) and choosing the **Friends except Acquaintances** option.

CHAPTER 5

Setting Your Status

Use Facebook's Status feature to share your thoughts and media with others. Learn how to tell friends about what you are up to, share links to content you have found online, ask questions, and upload images and videos to your page.

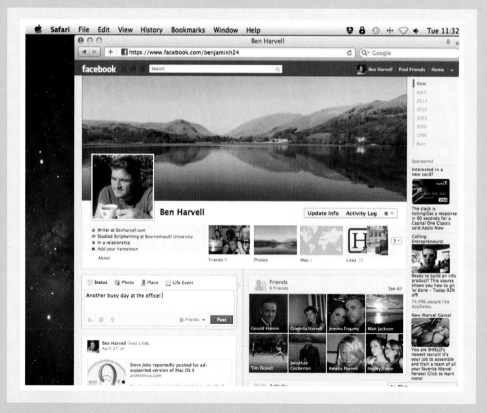

Update Your Status

Setting your status in Facebook can be as simple as typing how you are feeling and sharing it with all your Facebook friends. It does, however, offer more advanced options such as sharing links to websites and uploading video clips and photographs. Think of your status as your mouthpiece on Facebook that enables you to broadcast to all your friends who will see your updates on their news feed as well as on your timeline. When you update your status, friends can like or comment on the update or share any media or links you have included within it.

Update Your Status

① Click **News Feed** at the left of the Facebook interface.

The News Feed page appears.

② Click **Update Status** to show the status text box.

③ Click **What's On Your Mind?** and type your status message.

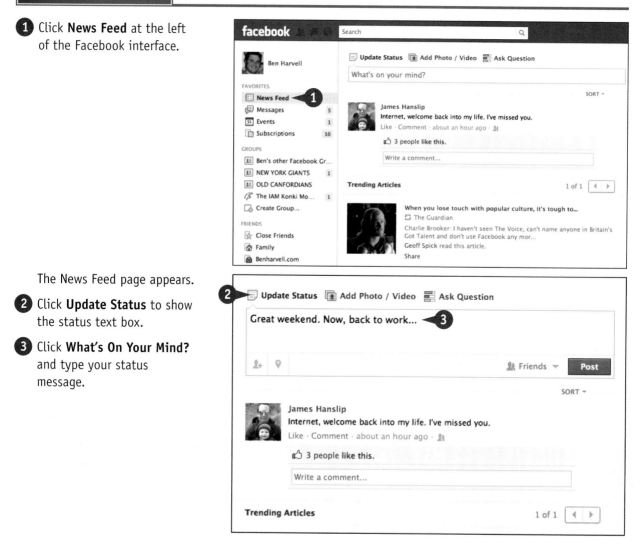

A Click the **Audience Selector** button (👥 Friends) and select who can see this message from the options menu.

4 Click **Post** to update your status.

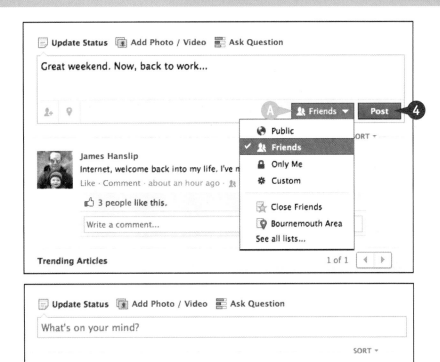

Your status now appears on your friends' news feed.

I made a spelling mistake in my update. How do I change it?
You cannot edit the text in a status after posting it. You can, however, edit the audience for an update, or delete the post completely. By deleting an update, you can replace it with a new, error-free status update. The easiest method for correcting an error is to copy the text from the original post, then delete that post and create a new update. You can then paste the original text into your new update and fix the error from the original before posting it.

Remove a Status Update

You can remove a Facebook status update after it has been posted. Facebook allows you to delete a status update you have already made directly from your news feed. This can be useful if you make a mistake in your update. The process is quick, and updates appear on your friends' news feeds as soon as you delete the update. The original update and all comments made on it will be removed.

Remove a Status Update

1 Locate a status update you have made on your news feed and position your mouse pointer over it.

An X appears at the right-hand side of your update.

2 Position your mouse pointer over the X to reveal the Delete Post message.

3 Click the **X**.

A dialog box appears with the option to delete your post.

4 Click **Delete Post**.

Facebook removes your post.

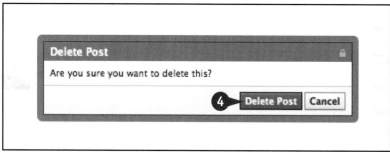

Edit a Status Update

If you post a Facebook update to the wrong group of people but do not want to delete it, you can make changes to it quickly from the news feed. For example, you may have made an update visible to the public but want only your friends to see it. By accessing the page dedicated to the update, which also includes any comments made on it, you can use the Audience Selector to adjust who can see the update. The changes take place immediately.

Edit a Status Update

1 Locate a status update you have made and click the link detailing the time it was posted, such as "about an hour ago."

A page containing your update appears.

2 Click the **Audience Selector** () at the top right of the update to reveal the options menu.

3 Click the group you want to allow to view your update.

Your edits to the status are updated on Facebook.

Share Uploaded Photos and Videos

You can upload photos and videos from your computer to share with friends on Facebook. This method enables you to quickly add a photo or video to your timeline that will appear on your friends' news feeds. You can also add a comment to your photo or video to explain it, and set privacy options to determine which of your friends can see the photo or video. This technique is useful for sharing photos or videos you have been sent via e-mail or movies you have edited on your computer.

Share Uploaded Photos and Videos

1 Click **News Feed**.

2 Click **Add Photo/Video**.

3 Click **Upload Photo/Video**.

4 Click **Choose File**.

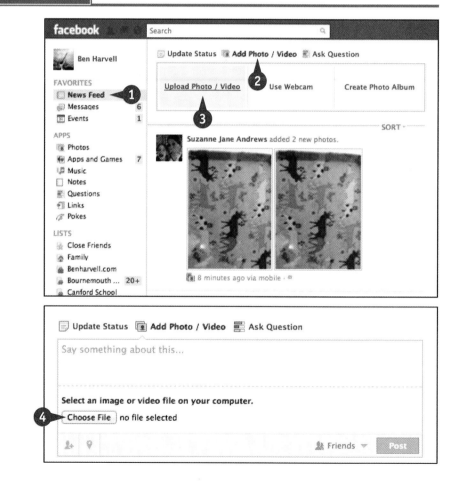

5 Select the photo or video you wish to share.

6 Click **Choose**.

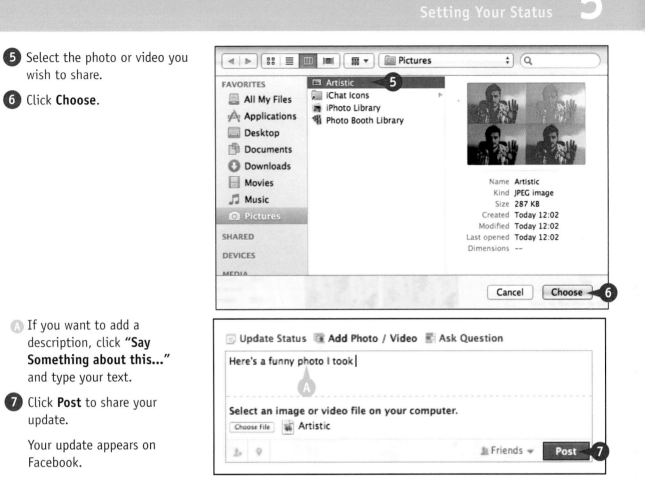

A If you want to add a description, click **"Say Something about this..."** and type your text.

7 Click **Post** to share your update.

Your update appears on Facebook.

TIPS

Can I tag people in the photos or videos I upload?

When your photo or video has uploaded to Facebook, you can use the location and tag buttons below the post to add a location and friends you are with. You can also use the Audience Selector to set who can see your photo or video.

Which video formats can I upload to Facebook?

Facebook caters for most popular video formats including AVI, MOV, MP4, MPEG, and WMV. It can also handle less common formats such as mobile video files as well as MKV, OGV, DAT, and DIVX files. You can find a full list of supported formats in the Facebook Help Center.

Share a Photo or Video from Your Webcam

I f your computer has a webcam built in or attached to it, you can share photos or videos you record with it from within Facebook. By selecting the **Use Webcam** option when sharing photos and videos, Facebook can connect to your webcam and use it to record video or take photos that you can immediately share with friends. The photo mode even allows for you to add fun effects to your images before you take the photo.

Share a Photo or Video from Your Webcam

1 Click **News Feed**.

2 Click **Add Photo/Video**.

3 Click **Use Webcam**.

If an Adobe Flash Player Settings dialog box appears, check the **Allow** option and click **Close**.

Note: Recording video using Flash, as in this task, can mean that it cannot be viewed on mobile devices like the iPhone and iPad. For full visibility it is better to record the video on your computer and upload it to Facebook as an AVI, MP4 or MPEG file.

A A preview image from your webcam appears on-screen.

4 Click the **Record** button at the bottom of the preview screen to begin recording video.

5 To take a photo, switch from Photo to Video mode by clicking the button at the top right of the preview.

The preview window switches
to Photo mode.

6 Click **No Filter** at the top left
of the preview window.

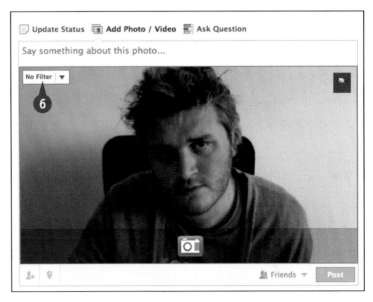

7 Select a filter from the
options menu.

8 Click the **Camera** button to
take your photo.

9 When you are happy with
your photo or video, click
Post to share it.

Why is there no sound recorded with my video?
You may not have the right microphone selected. Right-click (Control+click) on the video preview screen
and select settings from the pop-up menu. Click the **microphone** tab and select a microphone from the
menu. On this screen, you can also check if the recording volume is set to a high enough level to capture
sound through the microphone. If you still do not hear any sound, try using a different microphone or
revert to using your built-in microphone if your computer has one.

Ask a Question

Facebook Questions make it easy to receive quick advice and recommendations from friends. Questions do not have to be answered by your friends either; anyone can participate. However, answers from your friends are always listed first. You can ask a question from the news feed and select poll options to provide a choice of answers to your question. You can also allow friends to add their own answers to the question if you want to.

Ask a Question

1 Click **News Feed**.

2 Click **Ask Question**.

3 Click **Ask something...** and type your question.

A Click **Add Poll Options** to give people a choice of answers to your question.

4 Click the **Audience Selector** () and choose who to share your question with from the options menu.

5 Click **Post**.

Your question appears on your timeline and on news feeds of friends.

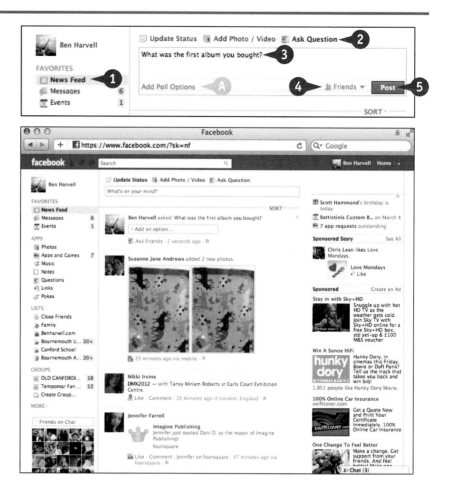

Browse Questions

Q uestions that your friends ask on Facebook appear in your news feed and can be answered from within your news feed, or you can click the question title to view a dedicated page for that question. You can also view all questions asked by your friends in chronological order on the Questions page to catch up on what your friends are asking. From this page you can answer and follow questions so that you are notified when others answer a question your friend has asked.

Browse Questions

1 Click **Home**.

2 Click **Questions**.

The Questions screen appears.

A Click **Your Activity** to see questions you have asked.

Follow a Question

Following a question means that you are subscribed to it and will receive notifications when somebody answers the question. Friends will see that you have subscribed to the question on their news feed. A question can be followed by clicking the **Follow** link beneath a question, and can be unfollowed at any time by clicking the **Unfollow** button. By following a question, you can see how many people share your view on a particular question and see the final number of answers to the question.

Follow a Question

1 Click **Home**.

2 Click **Questions**.

The Questions screen appears.

3 Click the **Follow** link beneath the question you want to follow.

You are now notified when friends answer the question you have followed.

Answer a Question

Answering a question allows you to cast your vote on a particular topic. Most questions include a list of possible answers from which to choose, and some allow you to add your own answers. You can also post comments on questions when viewing a page dedicated to a question to provide more detail on your answer. When you answer a question, your answer appears on the news feeds of your friends, and the person who asked the question is notified.

Answer a Question

1 Click the title of the question you want to answer.

Note: You can also click the title of a question on the Questions page.

A page for the question appears.

2 Click your preferred answer (☐ changes to ◉).

Note: Click **Add an answer...** if it is shown, to add your own answer, and click **Add**.

Ⓐ If you want to write a comment on the question, type into this field.

Share a Link

I f you find an interesting article on a website or want to point friends to a promotion, YouTube video, or literally any other location on the web, sharing a link is the way to do it. Facebook recognizes when you include a link in your status update and offers a number of display options to help your friends access the content you have shared. This includes the title of the link or web page and an image if one is available. You can set who will see the link you have shared, and friends can comment on the link and share it with their friends, too.

Share a Link

1 Click **News Feed**.

2 Click **Update Status**.

3 Click **What's on your mind?** and type or paste a website address into the update box.

Note: You can also add a link by dragging a URL from the address bar of most browsers into this field.

A Facebook recognizes the link and adds an additional section to your update with information about the link.

4 Click the arrows next to the image to select a thumbnail for your link.

Note: If only one or no image is available at the link you have shared, these arrows are grayed out and unusable. You can also check the **No Thumbnail** option (☐ changes to ☑) to show only text in your update.

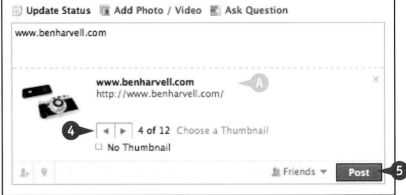

5 Click **Post**.

Like Content

iking content on Facebook lets your friends know what posts, photos, and updates you enjoy. Almost all items on your Facebook news feed provide a Like option. When you like content on Facebook, the person who posted the content is notified of your like, and the fact that you like the content is listed below it for your friends to see. Likes are also posted to your timeline so friends can see the content for themselves by clicking the link.

Like Content

1 Click **Like** below your chosen content.

The Like section expands.

(A) The number of likes and names of friends who like this content appear here.

2 Click **Write a comment** and type a comment into the field.

3 Press Enter (Return)

Your like appears on your timeline and on the news feeds of friends.

New York Giants
Hit the LIKE BUTTON to welcome Virginia Tech RB David Wilson to the Super Bowl Champion Giants! Watch LIVE reaction on Giants.com!

Like · Comment · Share · 21,864 · 1,223 · 602 · 6 hours ago

New York Giants
Hit the LIKE BUTTON to welcome Virginia Tech RB David Wilson to the Super Bowl Champion Giants! Watch LIVE reaction on Giants.com!

Unlike · Comment · Share · 21,870 · 1,221 · 603 · 6 hours ago

You and 21,869 others like this. (A)

View all 1,223 comments — 602 shares

Great pick! (2)
Press Enter to post your comment.

Like Content on the Web

Some websites include a Like button that works in the same way as the Like feature on Facebook. Like buttons can appear on content such as blog posts, videos, and advertisements, and you can like this content when outside of Facebook on another website. Content you like on the web appears on your timeline and on the news feeds of your friends. Liking some content on websites may mean you are liking a page, and therefore you are notified of updates to that page in future.

Like Content on the Web

1 Click **Like** (⟨👍 Like⟩) below any content on the web.

The Like button turns gray and a comment space appears.

2 Click the comment field and type a comment.

3 Click **Post to Facebook**.

Your like now appears on your timeline.

Note: Some Like buttons redirect you to your Facebook page to share a link.

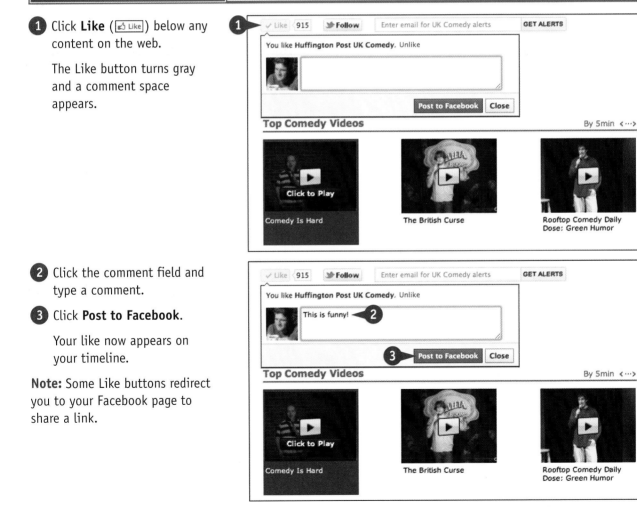

Turn On Subscriptions

Turning on Subscriptions allows others to subscribe to the content you make public. When others subscribe to you, they do not become your friend and you do not see posts from them. When you turn Subscriptions on, your friends are already subscribed to you, but others who are not your friends will also have the option to subscribe to your public posts. Subscriptions can be used to share information with people you do not know well enough to become friends with on Facebook, but who may still be interested in your updates. Users you have blocked, however, cannot subscribe to your updates.

Turn On Subscriptions

1 Click the Account menu (⊡).

2 Click **Account Settings** from the options menu.

The Account Settings screen appears.

3 Click **Subscribers**.

4 Click the **Allow Subscribers** box. (☐ changes to ☑).

A subscribe button now appears on your timeline and public profile.

Subscribe to a Person

Subscriptions offer you a way to be notified of public posts from people you do not follow on Facebook. These can be celebrities or simply people you are interested in. When you subscribe to a person, only posts he or she makes public are visible to you as a subscriber. You can also choose the type and frequency of updates you receive from people you subscribe to. You can set the frequency of updates at the point of subscribing or at a later stage. The subscribe button is found at the top right of the timeline for those who have subscriptions turned on.

Subscribe to a Person

1 Click the name of a person on Facebook.

The timeline for that person appears.

2 Click **Subscribe**.

The Subscribe button changes to Subscribed.

③ Position your mouse pointer over the Subscribed button.

An options menu appears.

④ Click **Settings**.

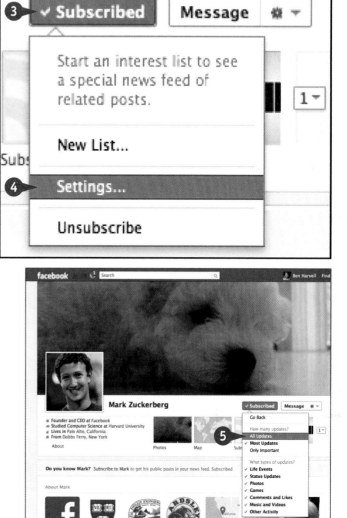

The Settings options menu appears.

⑤ Select how and what types of updates you receive by clicking options on the menu.

You are now subscribed to your chosen person.

How do I use the New List option on the subscription menu?
When you click **New List** on the subscription menu, you are given the option to select people, pages, and friends from which to create a feed containing all their updates. Lists appear in the left hand column of the Facebook interface and clicking on the list title will show only updates from those on the list. This can be a handy way to quickly access updates on a particular topic such as sports or music, by adding people you subscribe to, who regularly discuss those topics, to a list.

Find People to Subscribe to on Facebook

If you are looking to subscribe to people on Facebook, you can view a selection of suggested people in a list. These recommended subscriptions are based on the interests, likes, and subscriptions of you and your friends. Subscriptions are a good way to keep up to date with news from people you do not know such as celebrities or athletes. Only public updates from people you subscribe to are shown on your timeline, and you can set how many updates you receive.

Find People to Subscribe to on Facebook

1 Click **Subscriptions**.

Note: You may need to click **More** at the bottom of the left-hand column to reveal the Subscriptions link.

The Subscriptions page appears.

2 Click **See All** next to People To Subscribe To.

A list of recommended people to subscribe to appears.

3 Click **Subscribe** next to each person you want to subscribe to.

Unsubscribe from a Person

You can unsubscribe from someone you previously subscribed to very quickly by visiting his or her timeline and selecting the Unsubscribe option. When you unsubscribe from a person, you no longer see his or her public updates on your news feed or in any lists you have made that include the person. People you unsubscribe from do not receive a notification that you have unsubscribed. You can always subscribe to a person again at a later stage if you want.

Unsubscribe from a Person

1 On the timeline for the person from whom you want to unsubscribe, position your mouse pointer over the **Subscribed** button.

The Subscription options menu appears.

2 Click **Unsubscribe** from the options menu.

You are now unsubscribed from updates from this person.

CHAPTER 6

Communicating with Friends

You can communicate with friends on Facebook in a number of ways, from sending messages to using the Chat feature for instant messaging. You can also send e-mails with Facebook and make video calls.

Send a Message

Sending a message on Facebook works in the same way as it does in e-mail. You can select a friend to send a message to and, once the message is sent, Facebook notifies your friend of a new message, either on the site or via e-mail or text message if those notifications are set up. Your friend can then reply to the message, at which point you receive a notification, and a transcript of your past messages appears on the messages screen.

Send a Message

1 Click **Home**.

2 Click the **Messages** button (■).

3 Click **Send a New Message** from the Messages menu.

The New Message window appears.

4 Click the **To** field and type the name of a Facebook friend.

5 Click the **Message** field and type your message.

6 Click **Send**.

Your message is sent and the transcript of messages between you and your friend is shown.

TIPS

How will I know if a friend responds to my message?
When a new message arrives, a red circle appears over the **Messages** button (). If you have e-mail or text notifications turned on, you are also updated in an e-mail or as a message on your mobile phone.

How do I reply to a message from a friend?
Beneath the message from your friend is a text field. Click **Write a reply...** within that field and type your response. Click **Reply** to send your message.

View Your Messages

All the messages you receive on Facebook are collected on the Messages screen and listed chronologically. The Messages screen shows the friend who sent you a message or the friend you sent a message to, and the first line of the most recent message. You can also use the search field to look for messages if you have too many messages to scroll through. The Messages screen also shows messages among you and multiple friends if you are included in a conversation with a group of people.

View Your Messages

1 Click **Home**.

2 Click **Messages**.

The Messages screen appears.

A Click the name of a friend to view all messages in the conversation.

B Messages from a group of friends list all friends included and show a selection of profile pictures next to the message.

3 Click the search field and type your search criteria.

A list of messages appears.

④ Click the message you want to view from the messages menu.

Ben Harvell Home ▼

+ New Message   Q▼ Amelia

Amelia Harvell
I know! That's why I was asking! Reckon you can come home for a bit? Xx

See more results for Amelia ▶
Displaying top result

...e me mad! Was lookin...

...arring role in the Horri...   March 23 ○ ✕

...ke Chorizo Bread this ...   March 1 ○ ✕

...x   February 23 ○ ✕

The message transcript screen appears.

Amelia Harvell   ◂ Messages   ⚙ Act

Amelia Harvell   August 3, 2009
Oi Mr Elusive! Bathroom looks good. Now you're back online, pls can u get involved on iRecommend! Jons needs some more posts! Thanks, Beast xxx

Ben Harvell   August 3, 2009
Hi Beast,

Yeah, I saw his email but have been a bit busy with work. I'll do my best to get on there tonight and get involved.

Speak soon

x

Amelia Harvell   August 3, 2009
Thanks Benny! Lol xx

Amelia Harvell   August 10, 2009
Poor sleepy clown,de jour's given me his swine flu so feeling rough.Bathroom's looking good! Are we still on for bank hols weekend? Xx

Ben Harvell   August 8, 2011
Sorry, phone isn't playing nicely. All okay where you are? xx

Amelia Harvell   August 8, 2011
No
Sorry haven't finished! No, was having drinks in clapham junction & we were tols

Write a reply...   Reply

TIPS

Why are some of my messages highlighted in blue?
Messages highlighted in blue on the Messages screen have not been read yet. Highlighted messages you have read no longer appear blue until another new message arrives.

How do I delete messages?
Open the conversation that contains the message you want to delete and select **Delete Messages** from the **Actions** menu. Select the messages you want to delete (☐ changes to ☑) and click **Delete Selected** or **Delete All**.

Attach a File to a Message

When you send messages to friends on Facebook, you can attach a file from your computer as you would to an e-mail message. The file then is uploaded to Facebook and sent to your friend, who can then download it. You can attach any file format to a message, but the person who receives it needs the software required to open the file to view it. The larger the file size, the longer it takes for the file to upload and for the message to send.

Attach a File to a Message

1 Click **Messages** (■).

2 Click **Send a New Message**.

The New Message window appears.

3 Type the name of your friend and your message in the relevant fields.

4 Click the **Attach a file** button (📎).

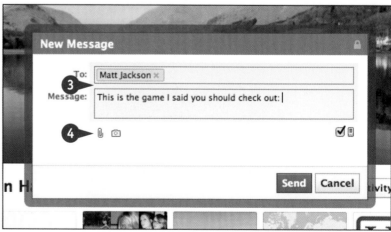

A browser window appears.

5 Select the file you want to attach and click **Choose**.

The file is attached to your message.

6 Click **Send**.

TIP

How do I delete an attachment?
Before you send your message, click the **X** next to the name of your attachment listed beneath your message. The attachment is removed from the message. You can now add a new attachment to your file, or you can send your message without an attachment.

Attach Photos and Videos to Messages

Using your webcam, you can take a photo or record a video and attach it to a message you send to a friend on Facebook. You need to have a built-in webcam or a webcam attached to your computer to use this feature. When a friend receives a photo or video attachment, he or she can view them on the Facebook Messages screen and send a response. It is important to note that some mobile devices, including the iPhone and iPad, may not be able to receive videos in messages.

Attach Photos and Videos to Messages

1 Click **Messages** (■).

2 Click **Send a New Message**.

The New Message window appears.

3 Type the name of your friend and your message in the relevant fields.

4 Click the **Take a picture or video** button (⊡).

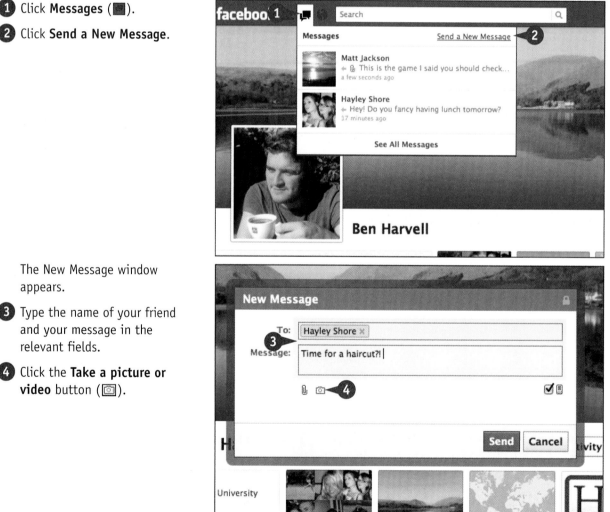

The photo interface appears.

A Click the **Switch to Video** button () to switch to video recording.

5 Click the **Camera** button (📷) to take a photo.

The camera counts down from three and takes a photo.

The photo or video is attached to your message.

6 Click **Send**.

TIP

How long can my video attachment be?

You can record up to twenty minutes of video when adding a clip as an attachment to a message. The longer you record, however, the longer the upload of the video takes. It also takes longer for the message to send because the video needs to be uploaded before sending.

Chat with Friends

Facebook includes a built-in instant messaging system that enables you to chat with friends from within the Facebook interface. The Chat menu lists your friends alphabetically and uses different symbols to show which of your friends are available to chat. A green dot (■) means that a friend is available to chat, and the phone icon (▯) means that a friend is using a Facebook app on a mobile device and may see your message. If no symbol appears next to a friend on the Chat menu, he or she is not available to chat.

Chat with Friends

1 Click **Chat** at the bottom right of the interface.

Note: If your browser window is wide enough, the Chat menu may already appear on the right of the screen.

The Chat menu appears.

A If you cannot find a specific friend, type his or her name into the Search field and press Enter (Return).

2 Click the name of an available friend on the list.

112

The chat interface appears.

3 Click the space at the bottom of the interface, type your message, and press **Enter** (**Return**).

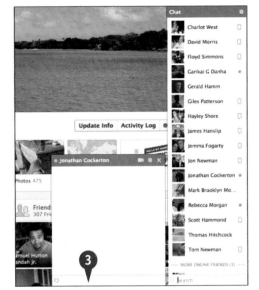

Your message is sent. Responses from your friend appear on the same interface.

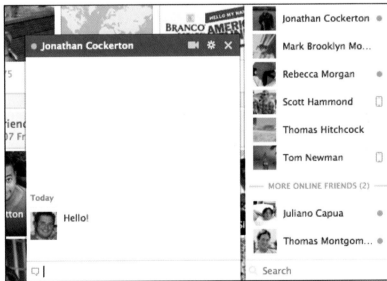

TIPS

What happens if I close the chat interface during a chat?
Your conversation remains live and the chat interface reappears if a new message is received. You can return to the chat you closed by clicking the name of the friend you were chatting with on the Chat menu.

How do I minimize the chat interface?
You can click the top of the chat interface to minimize it. The name of the person you were chatting to remains as a tab at the bottom of the screen.

Chat with Multiple Friends

You are not limited to chatting with only one friend through the Facebook Chat feature. You can add more friends to your conversation by using the **Add Friends to Chat** feature, which enables you to select other friends to add to the chat you are currently in. Friends are automatically added to the chat once selected, and receive messages from everyone in the same chat conversation. Every person added to the chat can view messages and send his or her own messages to the other members of the chat. All messages are shown within the chat interface.

Chat with Multiple Friends

1 Click **Chat** at the bottom right of the interface.

Note: If your browser window is wide enough, the Chat menu may already appear on the right of the screen.

The Chat menu appears.

A If you cannot find a specific friend, type his or her name into the Search field and press Enter (Return).

2 Click the name of an available friend on the list.

The chat interface appears.

③ Click the **Options (Action)** button (⚙).

④ Click **Add Friends to Chat** from the options menu.

A text field appears in the chat interface.

⑤ Type the name of the friend you want to add.

⑥ Click **Done**.

Ⓑ A new chat interface appears with both friends included.

TIPS

Can I add more friends to the chat?
You can continue to add friends to the chat by clicking the **Add more friends to chat** button (👥). Type the name of the friend you want to add and click **Done**.

Can I add multiple friends to a chat at once?
Yes. You can type multiple friends into the text field that appears when you click **Add Friends to Chat** or the **Add more friends to chat** button (👥).

Set Who Can See You on Chat

You can set which friends on Facebook can chat with you and those who cannot see your chat status by using the Advanced Settings menu. By default, all friends can see when you are available to chat, but you can hide your status from selected friends, lists, or everyone on Facebook. When hidden, the people from whom you selected to hide your chat status see you as not available when they view their Chat menu.

Set Who Can See You on Chat

1 Click the **Options (Action)** button (⚙) at the top of the Chat menu.

2 Click **Advanced Settings** from the options menu.

The Advanced Chat Settings window appears.

A Click **All your friends see you except** and type the names of friends or lists of friends to hide your chat status from.

B Click **Only some friends see you** and type names or lists into the field to select who can see you.

C Click **No one sees you (go offline)** to appear offline to everyone.

3 Click **Save**.

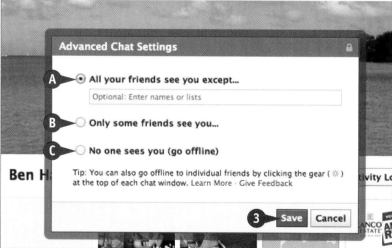

116

Turn Chat Sounds On or Off

By default, Facebook plays a sound when a new chat message is received or a video chat is initiated. These sounds can be switched on or off by using the Chat settings menu. You can hear chat sounds only if your computer has built-in speakers or speakers attached to it. You also need to ensure that your computer speakers are turned up so that you can hear the sounds when you have chat sounds turned on.

Turn Chat Sounds On or Off

1 Click **Chat**.

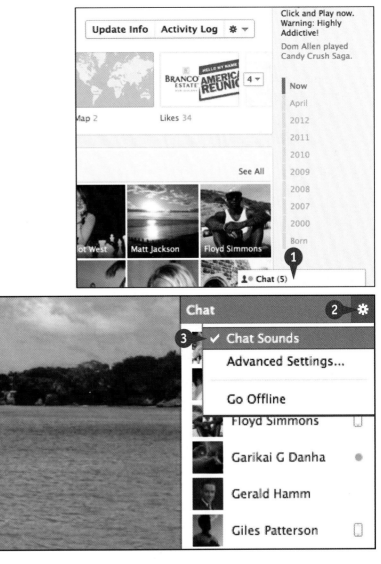

The Chat menu appears.

2 Click the **Options (Action)** button (⬛).

3 Click **Chat Sounds** from the options menu.

The check mark next to Chat Sounds disappears to denote that chat sounds are turned off.

Send Messages Through Chat

If you want to chat with a friend who is not available for chat, you can still send that friend a message using the chat interface. Your message appears to your friend in the same way as if you sent the message through the Messages screen; the friend receives a notification that your message has arrived. When your friend next logs in to Facebook, he or she can reply with a message from the Messages screen or through the chat interface.

Send Messages Through Chat

1 Click the name of a friend on the Chat menu who is not available.

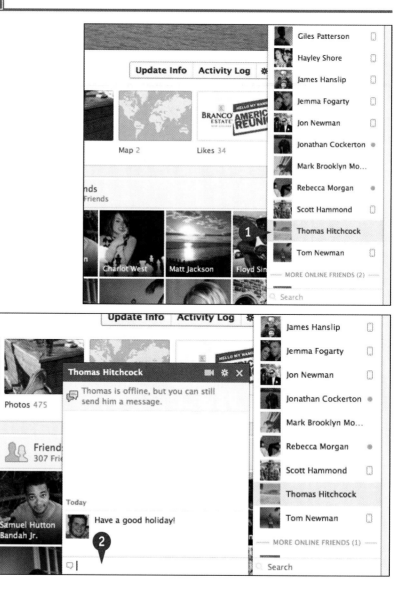

The chat interface appears with a message telling you that your friend is offline.

2 Click the message field, type your message, and press Enter (Return).

Facebook notifies your friend of your message when he or she next logs in to Facebook.

Send Facebook E-Mail

Your Facebook e-mail address is created from your Facebook username with the @facebook.com suffix applied. You must therefore set a Facebook username before using the address. When a username is set, people can e-mail you from any e-mail client using your @facebook.com address. You can also e-mail others using your @facebook.com e-mail address from the Messages screen. Facebook e-mail works like regular e-mail services and lists your messages in the same way as Facebook messages on the Messages screen.

Send Facebook E-Mail

① Click the **Messages** button (■).

② Click **Send a New Message** from the messages menu.

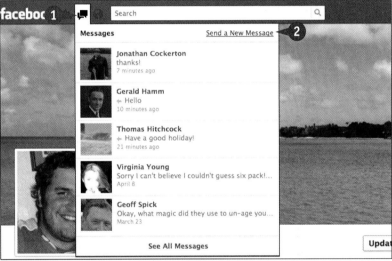

The New Message window appears.

③ Click the **To** field and type an e-mail address.

④ Click the **Message** field and type your message.

⑤ Click **Send**.

Facebook sends your message as an e-mail from your @facebook.com address.

Set Up Video Calling

You can make video calls to friends on Facebook using a webcam built in or attached to your computer. The first time you attempt to make a video call, you must complete a short setup process. This setup process happens only the first time you use video calling, and you can make video calls as soon as it is complete. If you use video calling on another computer, you may need to set up video calling on that computer as well. Some older computers may struggle with the video chat feature on Facebook as it requires the latest version of Adobe Flash Player in order to work. The same is true of mobile devices like the iPhone and iPad.

Set Up Video Calling

1 Click the **Action** menu (⚙▾) on the profile of a friend.

2 Click **Call** from the options menu.

A Set up Video Calling window appears.

3 Click **Install**.

A file now downloads.

4 Locate the downloaded file on your computer and run it.

Facebook Video Calling is installed and the call to your friend initiates.

Note: If you are running software that uses your webcam, such as Skype, you will need to close the application before using Facebook video calling.

TIPS

Can I use video calling via the Chat interface?
Yes. Click the **Video Calling** button (▣) on the chat interface to initiate a video call with the person you are chatting with.

What happens if I call a friend who has not installed Facebook Video Calling?
Facebook still places your call, but your friend is prompted to install Facebook Video Calling before he or she can answer the call. If you initiated the call from the chat interface, a message appears letting you know that your friend is setting up video calling.

Make a Video Call to a Friend

Once video calling has been installed on Facebook, you can call friends from the chat interface or from their timeline. When the video calling interface is shown, you can select the camera and microphone to use for the call and enlarge the video screen to full screen size if required. The first time you use video calling, you must complete a brief setup process if you have not done so already.

① Click the **Chat** button at the bottom of the Facebook interface.

② Click the name of the person to whom you want to chat.

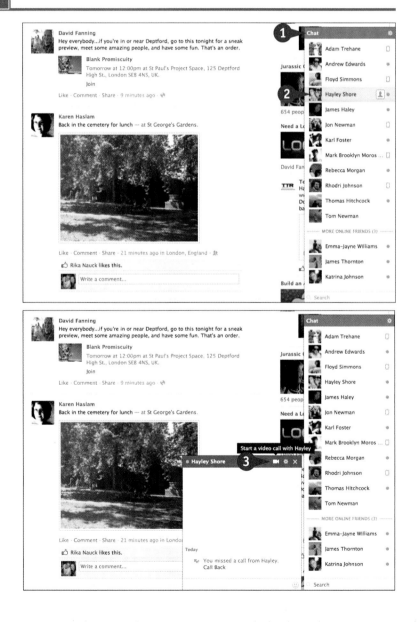

③ On the chat pane that appears, click the **Video Calling** button (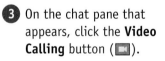).

Note: You can also call friends using the **Call** button on their Timeline.

122

A connection status window appears.

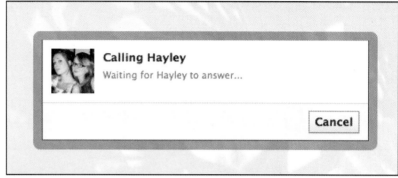

When your friend answers the call, the video calling pane appears.

A A preview of your video is shown at the corner of the screen.

B You can select a camera or microphone to use with video calling from the two menus at the bottom of the screen.

C To maximize the video call, click the **Maximize** button (⬚).

D To end the call, click the **Close** button (⬚).

TIP

My friend is not available to chat. Can I leave them a video message?
Yes. From your **News Feed**, click **Messages**. Click the **New Message** button and then click the **Take a Picture or Video** button (⬚). Now click the **Switch to Video** button (⬚) to record your video message. The video will be attached to your message and you can send it to any of your friends by adding their name to the **To:** field. It is worth noting, however, that some computers and mobile devices without Flash Player may not be able to view the video you send.

CHAPTER 7

Using Timeline and News Feed

The timeline and news feed are where most of the action happens on Facebook. Your timeline is a place for your friends to learn more about you and your interests, and your news feed is where you find out what your friends are up to.

Introducing the Facebook Timeline

The Facebook timeline offers a way for you to share your entire life in chronological order. Starting with your current activities, the timeline shows a selection of your photos, updates, and locations you have visited as well as major events in your life, such as relationships and marriages. You can edit your timeline to show exactly what you want and hide items you do not want shown. The timeline begins with a cover image of your choice and continues back through the years, finishing with your birth. Of course, you will likely have a big gap between when you were born and when you joined Facebook, but you can add events during this period to complete your timeline.

Timeline Cover and Information

The first image people see when visiting your timeline is your cover image. This large, wide photo can be any image from your Facebook photo library or uploaded from your computer. This image represents you and your interests, and should be colorful as well as big enough to fill the space without being stretched or distorted. Below your cover photo is your current profile picture and basic information as well as links to your Friends, Photos, Map, and Likes.

Timeline Stories

Stories on your timeline are memorable status updates, photos, likes, places, and relationships that cover major moments in your life. You can show, hide, and highlight stories on your timeline and also add events such as weddings, births, and new jobs at specific points. You add life events from the list of options at the top of the timeline. Stories make up a large part of your timeline and tell your story from birth to present day.

Timeline Apps

Any apps you use with Facebook, from online movie rental services to games and music players, can be included on your timeline. Updates from these apps, such as music you have listened to and runs you have tracked using Nike+, are added to your timeline and can be highlighted and hidden like regular stories. You are, of course, free to block apps from posting to your timeline by editing the app settings or simply hiding an update from an app on your timeline.

Timeline Privacy

The privacy settings you added to a story remain even when you include the story on your timeline, so only the people you wanted to share it with can see it. You can also use the View As feature to see how your timeline looks to others and how it will look to the public. If you want to remove an individual story from your timeline, you can quickly do so by clicking the edit button and selecting hide.

Introducing the Facebook News Feed

The Facebook news feed is your central hub for information from your friends and people you subscribe to. This is where all stories from your friends and subscribers appear, either by popularity or in chronological order, as well as comments on those stories. You can also see any changes your friends make to their account such as changing their profile picture or using apps. From the news feed you can comment on, like, and share stories as well as answer questions posted by your friends. You can also update your status and hide or remove stories on your news feed.

Add Your Own Stories

At the top of the news feed are options to update your status, upload media, and ask questions. Clicking any of the headings enables you to post content you want to share with your friends, and this information appears on their news feed as well as your own. Each story you send to the news feed can be set for a particular audience using the Audience Selector to determine which group of people can see it.

News Feed Stories

You can comment on, like, or share any story that appears on your news feed. Beneath each story is a set of links that, when clicked, enable you to do one of the above. Your like or comment is shown to friends as well as the person who added the story, and you can select a group of people to share a story with using the Audience Selector. For stories from a more specific group of people, you can use lists to show stories from selected friends or subscribers organized in the same way as the news feed.

Organizing the News Feed

You can organize the news feed in a number of ways to make sure you see the most important and most relevant content. At the top of the news feed, you can use the Sort feature to order stories by Top Stories or Most Recent. Facebook orders Top Stories by relevance using a number of factors to determine their importance. This includes the length of time since you last logged in to your account, how many comments and likes the post received, and your relationship with the person who posted the story.

Editing the News Feed

Stories you post to Facebook can be deleted from the news feed quickly by clicking the X at the top right of the post. Stories from friends and subscribers can also be hidden using the menu found at the top right of each post. This menu offers a number of options such as unsubscribing from a person, page, group, app, or event. Unsubscribing

from a specific type of update removes it from your news feed, and you will not receive any more stories of this type. You can also report spam stories from this menu. If you change your mind, you can use the Undo link to stop the action you just performed.

Add a Cover from Your Photos

The cover image is the first thing that people see when they view your timeline. The image acts as a large banner at the top of your timeline and appears behind your profile picture. Because the image appears fairly large and spans the width of your timeline, you should choose a picture big enough and that uses the right dimensions for it to appear properly. The width of the cover image should be at least 720 pixels. Some websites offer timeline images for download that you can use if you want.

Add a Cover from Your Photos

1 Click your name at the top right of the interface.

2 Click **Add a Cover**.

Note: If the Cover Photo information window appears, click **Okay** to continue.

3 Click **Choose from Photos** from the options menu.

The Choose From Your Photos window appears.

4 Click a photo from your recent uploads to use as a cover.

A To choose from another album, click **View Albums**.

Facebook adds the image to your timeline.

5 Click and drag the image to reposition it.

6 Click **Save Changes**.

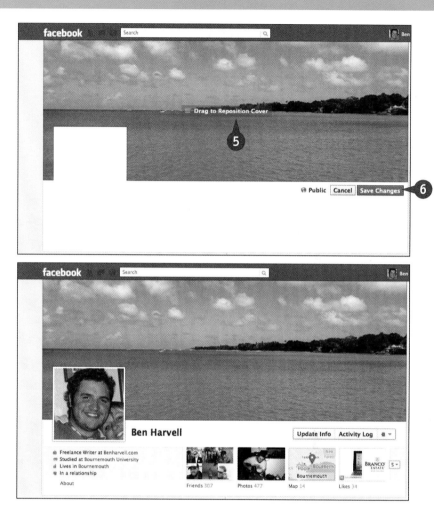

Your image is now set as your timeline cover.

Can I use any image as my timeline cover?
It is best to use an image you have uploaded to Facebook that sums you up or shows off your interests. Facebook does not allow images that advertise a product or service, or include indecent material. Commercial or copyrighted material or images already used on another timeline are also not allowed.

Upload a Cover Image

You can upload an image to use as your timeline cover rather than choose from your Facebook photos. The photo must be large enough to fit the width of your timeline and should be representative of you and your interests. After uploading the image, you can drag to reposition it to sit perfectly at the top of your timeline. Uploading an image allows you to choose a picture from another website or from your photo library on your computer.

Upload a Cover Image

1 Click your name at the top right of the interface.

2 Click **Add a Cover**.

Note: If the Cover Photo information window appears, click **Okay** to continue.

3 Click **Upload Photo** from the options menu.

A browser window appears.

④ Select an image on your computer.

⑤ Click **Choose**.

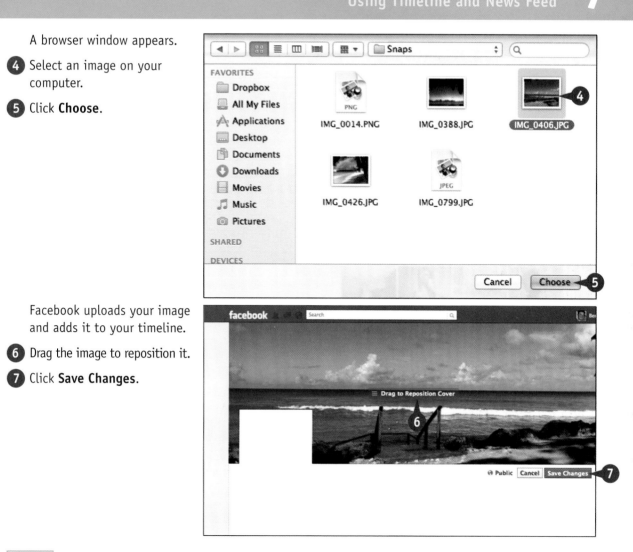

Facebook uploads your image and adds it to your timeline.

⑥ Drag the image to reposition it.

⑦ Click **Save Changes**.

Why does Facebook tell me to "Try a Different Image" when I try to upload a cover?
Your image is too small to be used as a timeline cover. The timeline cover image is displayed at 720 pixels wide, so the image you upload must be at least 399 pixels wide. Select a larger photo to upload, or use a higher-resolution version of the photo you want to upload.

Share Stories

If you particularly enjoy a story on your news feed, you can share it with your friends using the Share feature. Depending on the privacy settings set by the person who posted the story, you can use the Share feature to share the story with your friends or share it publicly so your subscribers can also see the story. When you share a story, you have the option to write a comment on it, and to set whom you share it with and where it will appear when you share it.

Share Stories

① Click **Share** below a story on your news feed.

The Share window appears.

② Click **On your own timeline** and choose where you want to share the story. Alternatively, leave the setting as it is to share it to your own timeline.

Note: If you select to share the story with a friend or a group, you must enter the name of the friend or group.

③ Click the **Audience Selector** (🛈 Friends) and select a group who can see the shared story.

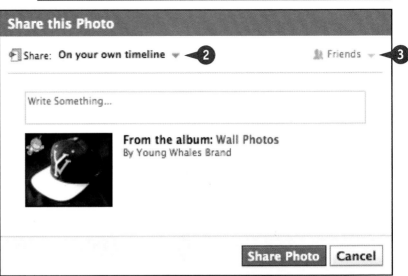

4 Click **Write Something** and type a comment in the field.

5 Click **Share**.

Note: The Share button changes depending on the type of content you are sharing, such as photos and links.

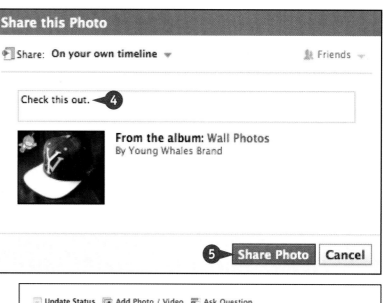

Share this Photo

Share: **On your own timeline** ▾   👥 Friends ▾

Check this out. ◀ 4

From the album: Wall Photos
By Young Whales Brand

5 ▶ **Share Photo** **Cancel**

Facebook shares the story on your timeline and makes it visible to the group you selected.

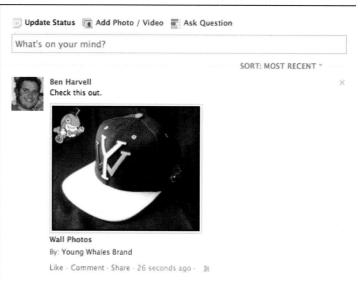

Update Status 📷 Add Photo / Video ❓ Ask Question

What's on your mind?

SORT: MOST RECENT ▾

Ben Harvell   ✕
Check this out.

Wall Photos
By: Young Whales Brand
Like · Comment · Share · 26 seconds ago · 👥

TIP

Where on Facebook can I share stories?
You can share a story to your own timeline where it will be visible to anyone who is allowed to view posts on your timeline. You can also share a story on the timeline of a friend so that their friends can see it. If you are a member of a group and have the required access level, you can post a story to a Facebook group. Finally, you can share a story on your Facebook page if you have created one.

Add Life Events to Your Timeline

Y ou can add a number of different life events to your timeline to show milestones such as marriages, births, holidays, and other significant events. By selecting a date and place, where applicable, the event is then added in its chronological position on your timeline. Life events can include a picture as well as a location, and can be set to appear to a select group of people using the Audience Selector.

Add Life Events to Your Timeline

1 On your timeline, click **Life Event**.

2 Click a Life Event category.

3 Click a life event.

Note: If a specific event is not listed, click **Other Life Event**.

The Life Event window appears.

4 Fill in event information by typing into the relevant fields.

A For some life events, you can also add friends you were with.

5 Click the arrows (⬍) and add years, months, and days from the pop-up menus.

6 Type a description of the event in the **Story** field.

7 Click **Choose from Photos**.

The Choose from Your Photos window appears.

8 Click an album, then click a photo within that album.

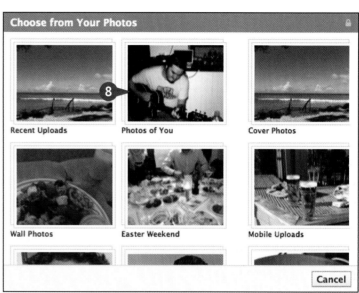

Choose from Your Photos

Recent Uploads

Photos of You

Cover Photos

Wall Photos

Easter Weekend

Mobile Uploads

Cancel

Facebook adds the photo to your event.

9 Click and drag the photo to reposition it.

10 Click **Save**.

Facebook adds the life event to your timeline.

The Barcelona Weekend
December 19, 2004 to December 22, 2004 with Matt Jackson
Visited Barcelona, Spain

What happens in Barcelona stays in Barcelona...

Trip Name   The Barcelona Weekend

Places Visited   Barcelona, Catalonia ×

From   2004 ◆   December ◆   19 ◆

To   2004 ◆   December ◆   22 ◆

With   Matt Jackson ×

Story   What happens in Barcelona stays in Barcelona...

✖ Remove...

Public ▾   Save   Cancel

TIP

How do I upload a picture to a life event?
On the Life Event window, click **Upload Photo** and select an image on your computer from the browser window that appears. Click **Choose**. Facebook uploads the picture and adds it to your event. When the picture has been added, you can click and drag it to move it into the position you want or you can click the red **X** to remove the picture from the event and upload a new one.

Add Photos to Your Map

The map found on your timeline automatically updates when you add life events, check in to locations, or include a location as part of a story. Each location is marked with a pin that, when clicked, shows relevant photos and events you have added to that location. You can add additional locations you have visited to the map, as well as add photos to a location. Facebook tags the photos you add to your map with the location, which appears when viewed on your photos page.

Add Photos to Your Map

1 Click **Map** on your timeline.

The Map screen appears.

2 Click **Add Photos to Map**.

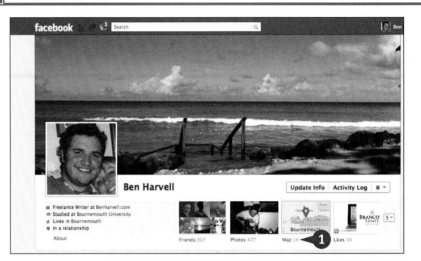

Your pictures appear above the map.

3 Click a photo.

A text field appears.

4 Type a location in the text field.

5 Click a location from the list that appears.

Facebook adds the location to the picture.

6 Click **Done Adding**.

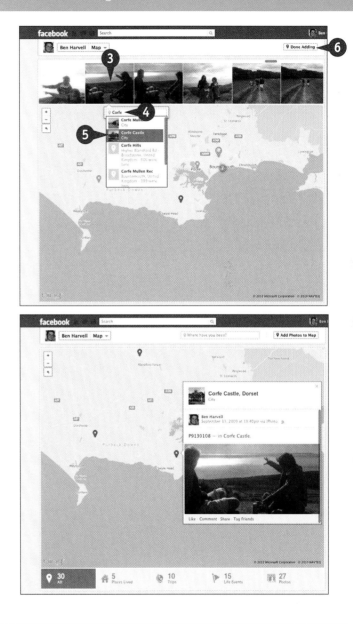

Pins appear on your map to show the photo locations.

Is there another way to add photos to the map?

Yes. When you upload a picture to Facebook there is a field within the details section that allows you to add a location to that picture. The location you add to the picture will be shown on the map once it has been saved. You can also add a location to images you have already uploaded to Facebook by clicking the **Add Location** button that appears when you view the photo in the photo viewer. From here you can type a location into the **Where was this photo taken?** field.

Hide and Highlight Timeline Stories

To better organize your timeline, you can choose to highlight and hide stories that appear on it. Highlighting a story makes it appear across the full width of your timeline and works especially well with photos. Hiding a story removes but does not delete it from your timeline, and, if a story is from an app, you can choose not to show posts from that app on your timeline in the future.

Hide and Highlight Timeline Stories

Highlight a Story

1 Position your mouse pointer over a story on your timeline.

The **Edit** (✎) and **Highlight** (★) buttons appear.

2 Click the **Highlight** button (★).

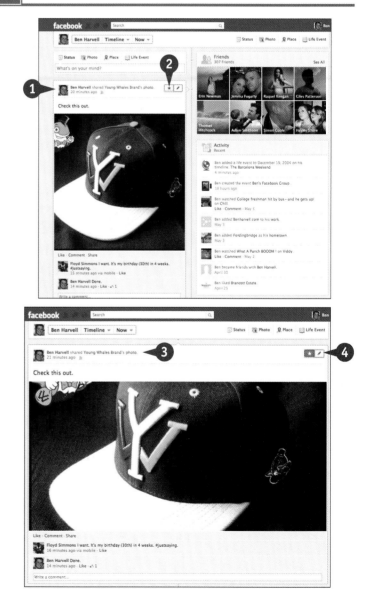

Facebook highlights the story.

Hide a Story

3 Position your mouse pointer over a story on your timeline.

The **Edit** (✎) and **Highlight** (★) buttons appear.

4 Click the **Edit** button (✎).

A pop-up menu appears.

 Click **Hide from Timeline**.

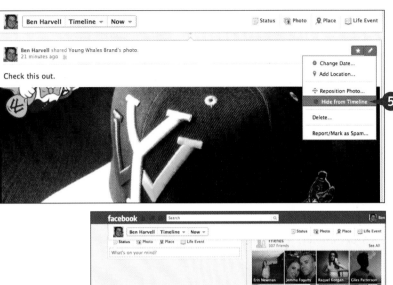

Facebook hides the story on your timeline. A message appears with the option to undo.

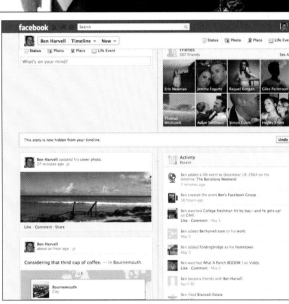

TIPS

How do I undo highlighting or hiding a story?
To remove a highlight from a story, simply click the **Highlight** button (⬜★) again. If you hide a story on your timeline, a placeholder that reads, "This story is now hidden from your timeline" appears in its place until you navigate away from your timeline. Click the **Undo** button on this placeholder to undo hiding the story.

Why can I not highlight some stories?
Some stories, including page likes and photo-tagging stories, cannot be highlighted and have to remain at their default size. Stories of this type do not have a **Highlight** button (⬜★) when hovered over with the mouse pointer.

Hide Stories on Your News Feed

You can hide stories that appear on your news feed and, if you do not want to see similar stories, set them to appear less frequently or not at all in the future. By hiding items on your news feed, you can make sure that the stories you see stay relevant to you and help Facebook to select the most relevant stories if you have your news feed set to show Top Stories.

Hide Stories on Your News Feed

1 Position your mouse pointer over a story on your news feed.

2 Click the arrow (∨) at the top right of the story.

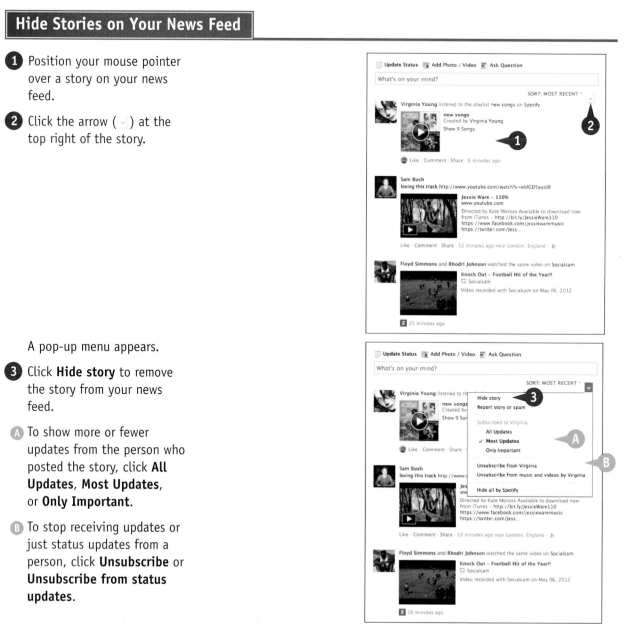

A pop-up menu appears.

3 Click **Hide story** to remove the story from your news feed.

A To show more or fewer updates from the person who posted the story, click **All Updates**, **Most Updates**, or **Only Important**.

B To stop receiving updates or just status updates from a person, click **Unsubscribe** or **Unsubscribe from status updates**.

Sort Stories on Your News Feed

You can organize the stories that appear on your news feed in two ways. The first is by Top Stories. Top Stories orders stories by their importance to you. Facebook determines the importance of a story by a number of factors, including your relationship to the person posting the story and the number of likes and comments it has received. The second method of sorting is Most Recent. Most Recent sorting simply organizes your news feed in chronological order.

Sort Stories on Your News Feed

1 Click **Sort** at the top right of your news feed.

A menu appears.

A Click **Top Stories** to show stories that Facebook believes to be important to you.

B Click **Most Recent** to show stories in chronological order.

Comment on a Story

When a friend or a person you subscribe to posts a story, you can make a comment on that story. Facebook adds your comment to the list of comments made on that story and makes it visible to everyone who can see the story. Comments enable you to add your thoughts to a particular story and add more detail than simply liking it. Facebook notifies the person who posted the story when your comment is added.

Comment on a Story

1 Click **Comment** below a story on your news feed.

Your profile picture appears next to the comment field.

2 Type your comment and press Enter (Return).

Hide and Adjust the Ticker

The ticker shows real-time information from your friends, including their likes, changes to their timeline, comments, and other updates. When viewed in a wide browser window, the ticker appears down the right of the page; when the browser window is smaller, the ticker appears at the top right corner of the screen. You can adjust the size of the ticker, and you can also completely hide the ticker if you want.

Hide and Adjust the Ticker

Adjust the Ticker Size

1 Click and drag the gray bar at the bottom of the ticker up or down to increase or decrease its size.

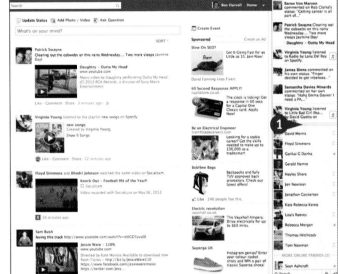

2 Decrease the size of your browser window to show the ticker at the top right of the interface or in a separate pane.

Hide the Ticker

3 Click the **Hide Ticker** button at the top right corner of the ticker.

Facebook hides the ticker.

CHAPTER 8

Using Groups and Events

Groups and events help you organize friends and colleagues on Facebook. Using groups, you can gather friends to discuss a specific interest and chat as a group, and with events you can plan and invite friends to events.

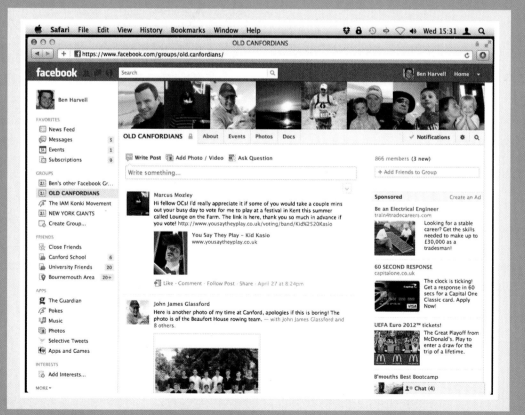

Join a Group

To join a group you must first ask to be invited, or if the group is a closed group, a group member or administrator must invite you. Open groups allow people to join at any time. A third type of group, secret groups, do not appear in searches and you cannot ask to join them. The only way you can join a secret group is for an existing member to invite you.

Join a Group

1 Find a group you want to join and click its title.

Note: You can find groups on your news feed or by using the Search box at the top of the screen.

The group page appears.

2 Click **Join Group**.

Facebook sends your request to join the group.

Note: You can cancel your request by clicking **Cancel Request,** which appears when you click **Join Group**.

Post to a Group

When you join a group, you can post updates; share links, videos, and photos; or ask a question of all members of the group. All group members see your post unless they have changed their settings to stop receiving updates from groups. They can still view your post when they access the group page. You can add your current location as part of your post and also tag other group members if you want.

Post to a Group

1 On the group page, for the group to which you want to post, click **Write Post**.

Note: You can also click **Add Photo/Video** or **Ask Question**.

The post area expands.

2 Type your update into the **Write Something** field.

A Click the **Tag** button (👤) to include other group members.

B Click the **Location** button (📍) to include a place.

3 Click **Post**.

Facebook sends your post to the group.

Create a Group

You can create a group on Facebook to which you can add your friends. The group could be for a club, work colleagues, or simply as a forum for a selection of your friends to communicate and share photos and videos with one another. Privacy settings allow you to make the group Open and therefore visible to anyone, Closed so that people can see the group but not the posts within it, or Secret so that only members can see the group and its posts.

Create a Group

1 Click **Home**.

2 Click **Create Group**.

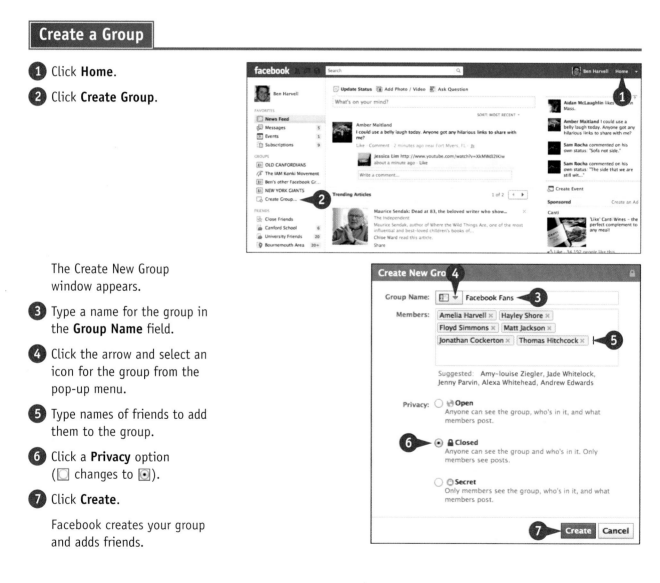

The Create New Group window appears.

3 Type a name for the group in the **Group Name** field.

4 Click the arrow and select an icon for the group from the pop-up menu.

5 Type names of friends to add them to the group.

6 Click a **Privacy** option (☐ changes to ☉).

7 Click **Create**.

Facebook creates your group and adds friends.

Search within a Group

You can search for specific names or topics within a group you are a member of by using the search field located in the bar that runs across the top of the group page. This allows you to look for posts and comments within the group that include your search criteria. Search results appear on a separate page, and you can quickly view the post you are looking for by clicking it.

Search within a Group

1 Click the **Search** button at the top right of the group page.

The Search This Group field appears.

2 Type your search into the field and press **Enter** (**Return**).

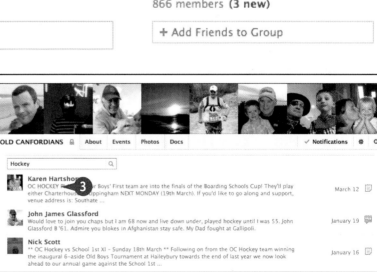

The search results screen appears.

3 Click a result to see the post that includes your search criteria.

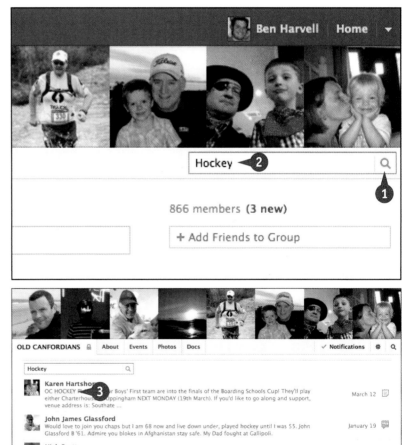

151

Add Friends to a Group

When you have become a member of a group or created one yourself, you can add friends to it using the Add Friends to Group feature. This small pane at the top right of the group page enables you to type the name of friends you want to add to the group. They then become members of the group after the owner or administrator of the group approves them. Friends can always remove themselves from the group at a later date if they want to.

Add Friends to a Group

1 On a group page, type the name of a friend into the **Add Friends to Group** pane and press Enter (Return).

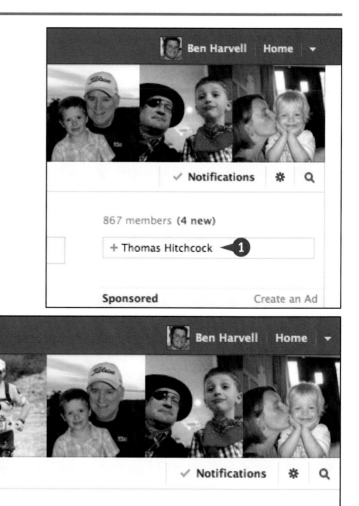

Facebook adds your friend or friends to the group pending approval from an administrator.

View Your Event Invites

When someone invites you to an event, you receive a notification and Facebook adds the event to your list of event invites. On your Events page, you can see all events you have been invited to as well as upcoming birthdays. Facebook organizes events in order of those happening soonest and shows the picture of the person who invited you, unless the event has an image assigned to it. You can view the event in more detail by clicking its title.

View Your Event Invites

1 Click **Home**.

2 Click **Events**.

The Events screen appears.

A Events you have been invited to as well as birthdays are listed by date.

Search Your Events

From your Events page you can quickly switch to alternate views of your events, including past events, birthdays, suggested events, and declined events. If you have many event invites, using the search filter to show only a specific set of invites can help you to find the event you were looking for. When you finish searching, you can move back to the Upcoming Events display to show the events coming soon to which you have been invited.

Search Your Events

1 Click **Home**.

2 Click **Events**.

The Events screen appears.

3 Click the **Search** button (🔍▾).

The Search pop-up menu appears, listing your events.

Ⓐ Click **Past Events** to show events that have already happened.

Ⓑ Click **Declined Events** to show events you did not attend.

Ⓒ Click **Birthdays** to show a list of birthdays for your friends.

Respond to an Event Invite

When you receive an event invite, you have three response options found on the event page: Join, Maybe, and Decline. Selecting Join means you will be attending the event and that you will receive notifications when the event is updated or people comment on the event. Clicking Maybe includes you in the event and comments on the event, but does not commit you to attending the event. If you decline the event, you receive no further updates from the event.

Respond to an Event Invite

1 Click **Home**.

2 Click **Events**.

3 Click the name of an event to which you have been invited.

Ⓐ You can also join or decline an event from the Events page by clicking the **Join** or **Decline** links.

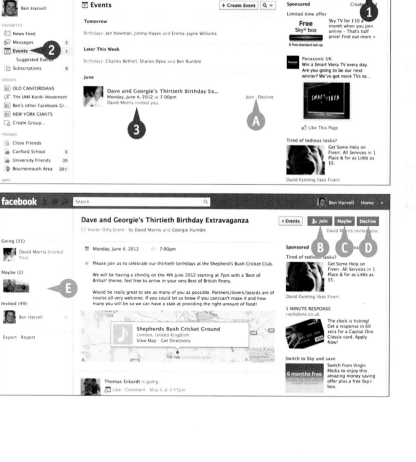

The event page appears.

Ⓑ Click **Join** to confirm your attendance and join the event group.

Ⓒ Click **Maybe** to let friends know you may attend.

Ⓓ Click **Decline** if you are not attending the event.

Ⓔ The list of guests appears on the left. You can click each section to view who will and will not be attending the event.

Export Events

I f you use an external calendar on your computer or on the web, you can add your Facebook events to it by exporting them from Facebook and then adding them to your chosen calendar application or service. All information on your Facebook calendar at the point of exporting can then be added to your calendar application. You will have to export your Facebook events again if new events are added. You can use Apple iCal, Microsoft Outlook, and Google Calendar among other applications to export your events by using a link that you can find on the Events page.

Export Events

1 Click **Home**.

2 Click **Events**.

3 Click the **Search** button ($\boxed{\mathsf{Q \vee}}$).

4 Click **Export Events** from the pop-up menu.

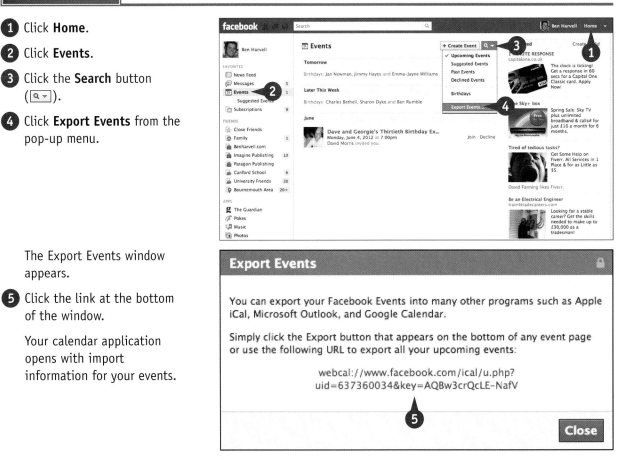

The Export Events window appears.

5 Click the link at the bottom of the window.

Your calendar application opens with import information for your events.

Export Events

You can export your Facebook Events into many other programs such as Apple iCal, Microsoft Outlook, and Google Calendar.

Simply click the Export button that appears on the bottom of any event page or use the following URL to export all your upcoming events:

webcal://www.facebook.com/ical/u.php?
uid=637360034&key=AQBw3crQcLE-NafV

Close

Find Suggested Events

Facebook determines suggested events depending on the events your friends are attending, places you have checked in to using a mobile device and the Facebook app, apps you use, and pages you have liked on Facebook. The list of suggested events is sorted with the soonest event listed first, and each event shows which of your friends are attending. You can choose to attend events on the Suggested Events screen or on the event page. When you confirm your attendance at an event, the admin of the event will be notified and your friends will see the update on your timeline and on their news feeds.

Find Suggested Events

1 Click **Home**.

2 Click **Events**.

3 Click **Suggested Events**.

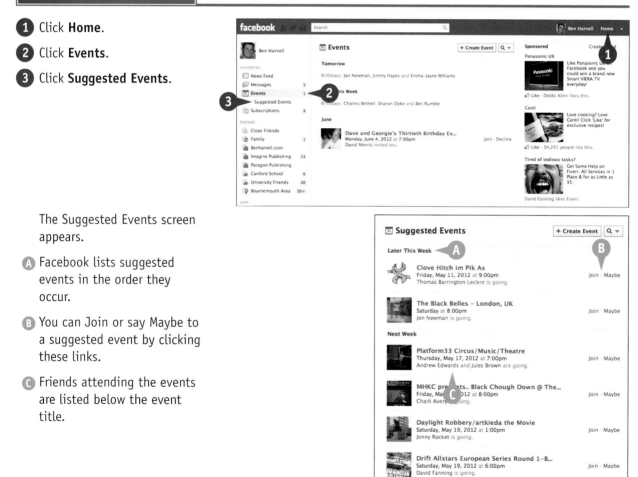

The Suggested Events screen appears.

A Facebook lists suggested events in the order they occur.

B You can Join or say Maybe to a suggested event by clicking these links.

C Friends attending the events are listed below the event title.

Invite Members of a Group to an Event

As well as creating an event for friends on Facebook, you can also create an event within a group. Creating an event within a group is a little different from a regular event because it includes privacy settings and invite options specific to the group for which you create the event. You can quickly invite all members of the group to the event and allow only members of the group to see the event. This is ideal for planning an event that you only want group members to be a part of or for work-related events.

Invite Members of a Group to an Event

1 Click **Home**.

2 Click the name of your group.

3 Click **Events**.

4 Click **Create Event**.

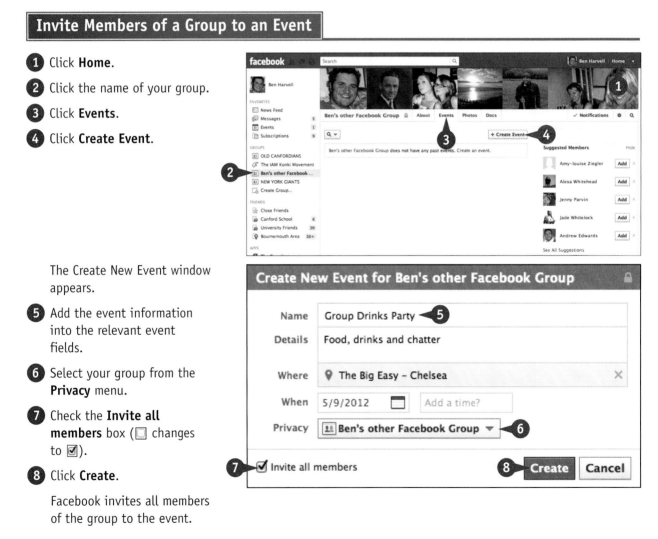

The Create New Event window appears.

5 Add the event information into the relevant event fields.

6 Select your group from the **Privacy** menu.

7 Check the **Invite all members** box (☐ changes to ☑).

8 Click **Create**.

Facebook invites all members of the group to the event.

Add Hosts to Your Event

As the creator of an event, you automatically become a host, but you can also add other friends as hosts to help you manage the event. Hosts can invite people to the event and edit the event information. Hosts can also add more hosts if they want. You can add hosts to your event quickly from the Edit screen within your event. It is best to only add those people who are interested in managing your event as a host or you may end up with too many people making changes to the event which can become confusing.

Add Hosts to Your Event

① Within your event, click the **Edit** button ([✎ Edit]).

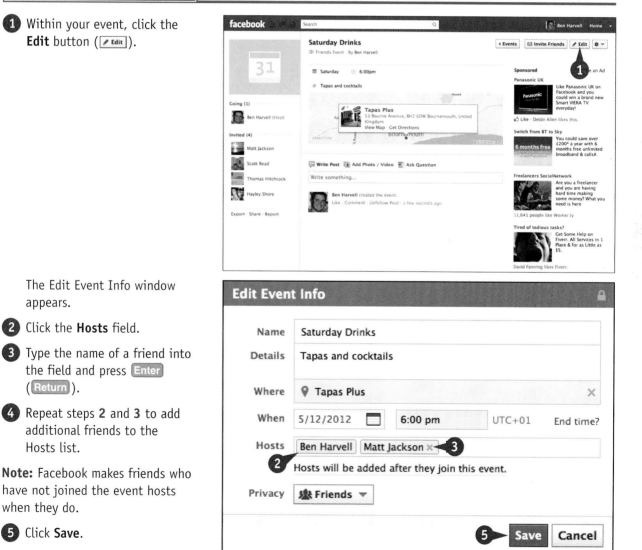

The Edit Event Info window appears.

② Click the **Hosts** field.

③ Type the name of a friend into the field and press (Enter) ((Return)).

④ Repeat steps **2** and **3** to add additional friends to the Hosts list.

Note: Facebook makes friends who have not joined the event hosts when they do.

⑤ Click **Save**.

Facebook makes the friends you added hosts for the event.

Add a Photo to an Event

If you do not add a photo to your event, Facebook displays your profile picture next to the event's title when others view it. You can set a photo for your event, however, which will appear in place of your profile picture. The image should represent the event and appears next to the title of the event as a thumbnail and on the main event page at the top left of the screen.

Add a Photo to an Event

1 Click the **Action** menu (⚙▾) on your event page.

2 Click **Add Event Photo**.

The Add Event Photo window appears.

3 Click **Choose File**.

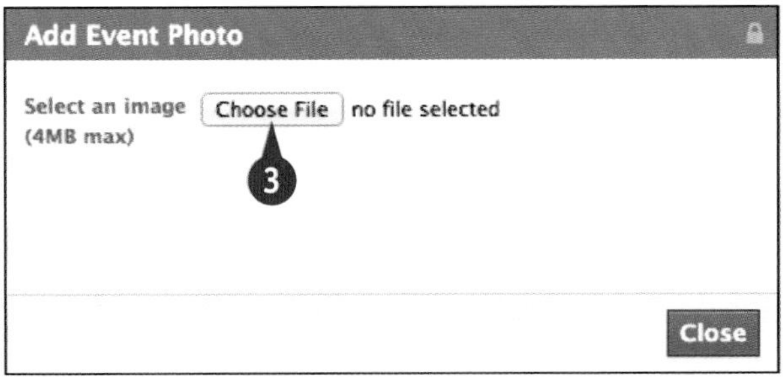

A browser window appears.

4 Click the photo you want to use.

5 Click **Choose**.

Facebook adds the photo to your event.

Chat with a Group

When you create your own group, you can chat with all the available group members at once using the Chat with Group feature. This initiates a Facebook chat conversation between you and every member of the group available to chat at that time. Chatting with a group works in the same way as chatting with multiple friends, and only members of the group can see the transcript of the chat.

Chat with a Group

1 Within a group you have created, click the **Action** menu (⬚▾).

2 Click **Chat with Group**.

A new chat window appears.

3 Type a message into the chat field and press Enter (Return).

Facebook sends your message to all available group members via chat.

Create an Event

By creating an event on Facebook, you can invite friends and family to real-world occasions. You can add a date, time, and location to an event, and invited friends can RSVP to your event on Facebook. Once you create an event and invite friends to it, Facebook notifies those invited when the event details change and when people comment on the event page. As the creator of an event, you can update event information at any time.

Create an Event

1 Click **Home**.

2 Click **Events**.

3 Click **Create Event**.

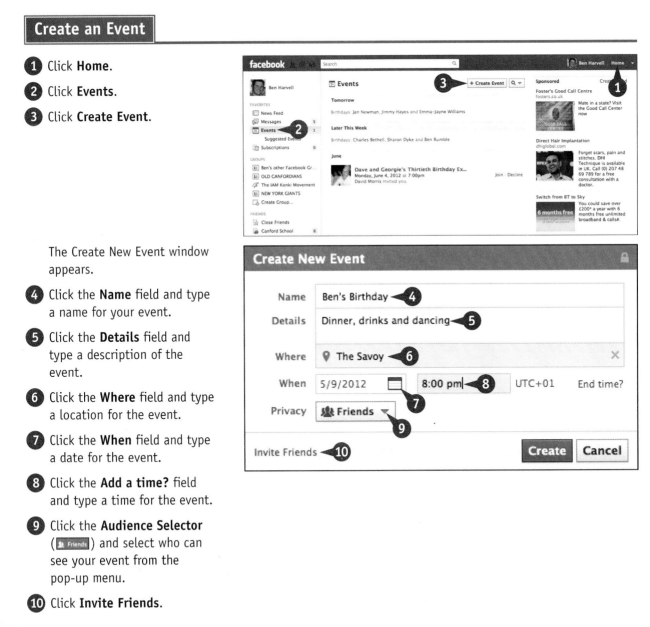

The Create New Event window appears.

4 Click the **Name** field and type a name for your event.

5 Click the **Details** field and type a description of the event.

6 Click the **Where** field and type a location for the event.

7 Click the **When** field and type a date for the event.

8 Click the **Add a time?** field and type a time for the event.

9 Click the **Audience Selector** (🔹 Friends) and select who can see your event from the pop-up menu.

10 Click **Invite Friends**.

The Invite Friends window appears.

11 Click the name of each friend you want to invite.

A You can search friends, lists, and groups using the search field.

12 Click **Save**.

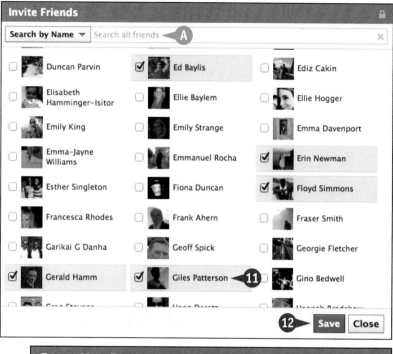

The number of friends you have invited appears at the bottom of the window.

13 Click **Create**.

Facebook creates your event and invites the friends you selected.

<hr/>

TIPS

Who can see my event when I create it?
Who can see your event depends on the privacy setting you choose. The Friends setting allows all your friends to see the event; the Public setting allows anyone to see your event; and the Invite Only setting makes your event visible only to those invited to it.

How do I set an end time for my event?
Click the **End Time** link on the **Create New Event** box and type an end time for your event into the field that appears.

163

CHAPTER 9

Sharing Photos, Video, and Music

On Facebook, you can upload photos and videos from your computer to share with friends on Facebook. You can also discover the music your friends are listening to and listen along with them by using music apps on Facebook.

Upload Photos to Facebook

You can upload multiple images from your computer to Facebook to create an album. Once you select the images you want to upload, you can then add a name, tags, locations, and dates to the album you are uploading. You can also add information for individual images within an upload and tag people in your photos by clicking their faces and typing their names. You can make changes to the album while photos are uploaded in the background.

Upload Photos to Facebook

1 Click **Home**.

2 Click **Photos**.

3 Click **Upload Photos**.

A file browser window appears.

4 Select the photos you want to upload.

5 Click **Open**.

The album creation window appears.

6 Click the album title and type a new album name.

7 Click the album description and type your comments.

8 Click **Where were these taken?** and type a location.

A To add a specific date to your photos, click **Add Date**.

B To add comments to individual photos, click this space and type a comment.

C You can add tags, dates, and locations to individual photos using these buttons.

D Click the **High Quality** box (☐ changes to ☑) to share large images at high quality.

E A blue bar shows the upload status.

9 Click **Post Photos**.

Your photos are added to your Facebook timeline and Photos page and will appear on the news feeds of friends.

TIPS

What if I upload the wrong pictures?
You can remove a photo from your upload by positioning the mouse pointer over it and clicking the button that appears. You can now select **Remove this photo** from the options menu.

How do I set a cover image for an album?
Select the picture you want to make the cover image for the album and click the options button. From the options menu, click **Make album cover**.

Upload Videos to Facebook

You can upload videos from your computer to Facebook and add information to them in the same way as you do photos. Videos take longer to upload than photographs and it depends on your Internet connection and the length of the video as to how long the upload and processing takes. Videos you upload must be under 1024MB and under twenty minutes in length and should be your property and without containing copyrighted material. Videos uploaded in this way may not be playable on mobile devices such as iPhones and iPads.

Upload Videos to Facebook

1 Click **Home**.

2 Click **Photos**.

3 Click **Upload Video**.

The Create a New Video screen appears.

4 Click **Choose File**.

A file browser window appears.

5 Select the video you want to upload.

6 Click **Choose**.

The video starts uploading.

7 Type a title for your video into the **Title** field.

8 Type where the video was taken into the **Where** field.

9 Type a comment into the **Description** field.

10 Click **Save Info**.

When the upload completes, Facebook adds your video to your timeline.

TIPS

Can I record video to Facebook with my webcam?
Yes. On the **Create a New Video** page, click **Record Video** and then click the record button to begin recording your video.

How do I e-mail videos to Facebook?
On the **Create a New Video** page, click **Mobile Video**. The e-mail address for video and photo uploads appears. Send videos as an e-mail attachment to this address to upload them to your Facebook account.

Organize Your Albums

Clicking the **My Albums** button enables you to see all the photos you have uploaded to Facebook organized by album. You can change the position in which albums appear on your albums page by clicking and dragging them. You can also set who can see a particular album by using the Audience Selector button. The privacy of some albums cannot be changed, such as Cover Photos, because they must remain public. You will also need to change individual privacy settings for photos in your Mobile Uploads and Webcam Photos albums.

Organize Your Albums

1 Click **Home**.

2 Click **Photos**.

3 Click **My Albums**.

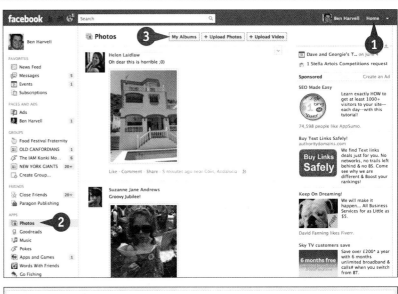

Your photos screen appears.

A Click and drag an album to move it to a new position on the page.

B Click the **Audience Selector** (🔽) on an album to select who can see it.

C Click **See More** to view more albums.

Tag Photos and Videos

You can tag photos on Facebook with the names of friends and family. In the photo viewer, the **Tag Photo** button changes the interface to allow you to click on people in a photo and add their name. Facebook notifies people you tag of the action and gives them the chance to untag themselves if they want to. When you are tagged in a photo, friends see the update on their news feed.

Tag Photos and Videos

1 When viewing an image in the photo viewer, click the **Tag Photo** button.

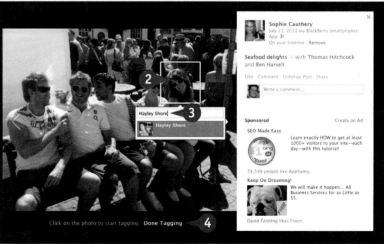

The mouse pointer changes to a crosshair.

2 Click the face of a person in the photo.

A text box appears.

3 Type a name into the box and press Enter (Return).

4 When you have finished adding tags, click **Done Tagging**.

Edit Uploaded Photos

You can edit photos you upload to Facebook at any time from the photo viewer. By clicking **Edit** for a photo, you can add and remove information including tags, description, location, and date. You can also click the **Audience Selector** button to set who can see the photo you are editing.

Edit Uploaded Photos

Edit basic information

1 Click one of your photos anywhere within Facebook.

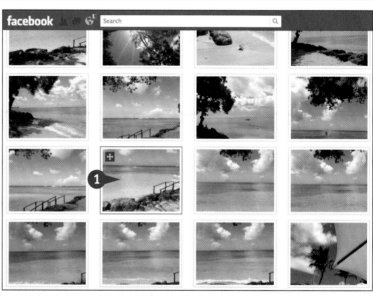

Your photo appears in the photo viewer.

2 Click **Edit**.

3 Click the description to add to it, or type a new description.

4 Click the X to remove a tag, or type more names to tag people.

5 Click the X to remove the location or type a new one.

6 Use the arrows (⬍) to change the date from the pop-up menu.

7 Set who can see the photo by clicking the **Audience Selector** (👤) and selecting a group from the options menu.

Use the Options Menu

8 Click **Options** below an image in the photo viewer.

Ⓐ Click **Rotate Left** or **Rotate Right** on the options menu to rotate the image.

Ⓑ Click **Download** on the options menu to download the image.

Ⓒ Click **Make Profile Picture** to set the image as your profile photo.

Ⓓ Click **Delete This Photo** to delete the image.

9 Click **Done Editing**.

Facebook saves your changes.

TIPS

Can people see photo metadata when they download my images?

No. Facebook does not include metadata information when people download your photos. Metadata is used only for determining a location when you upload an image.

Are the editing settings the same for my videos?

Videos have a number of similar editing options, including the option to tag and remove videos as well as change the location and description. You can also opt to embed a video from Facebook on a website or other social network.

View Photos Uploaded by Friends

Photos from your friends appear on your news feed when the images are posted or shared with you. You can also view photos from friends by clicking **Photos** from the left column. When you click a specific photo, the photo viewer appears and enables you to browse one photo at a time as well as like and tag the photos. To view an entire album of photos from a friend, click the album title to be taken to the album page, which includes a thumbnail of every photo in the album.

View Photos Uploaded by Friends

① Click **Home**.

② Click a photo uploaded by a friend.

The photo viewer appears.

③ Click the photo or arrows to see more images in the album.

④ Click the album name to view all photos in this album.

Review Photos You Are Tagged In

When you have Tag Review turned on, Facebook sends you notifications when a friend tags you in a photo. By accessing the photo in which you are tagged from the notifications menu, you can choose to approve or reject the tag and view other photos in which you have been tagged that are pending approval. Your friends on Facebook can see the tags you approve but not the ones you reject.

Review Photos You Are Tagged In

1 Click the **Notifications** button.

2 Click a notification for photo tags.

The photo opens in the photo viewer with the pending tags shown.

3 Click the check mark to approve the tag.

Ⓐ Click the X to reject the tag.

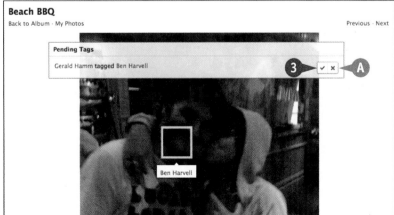

Set an Album Cover Image

Facebook automatically selects a cover image for albums of photos you upload. You can change this image by editing the album and selecting a new image as the cover. Facebook then shows this image when your album appears on your photos page or when it appears on the news feeds of your friends. You can change the cover image for an album at any time.

Set an Album Cover Image

1 Click the title of one of your photo albums.

The album page appears.

2 Click **Edit Album**.

3 Click the options menu button on a photo.

4 Click **Make album cover**.

5 Click **Done**.

Set a Video Thumbnail

Facebook automatically shows a thumbnail image for an uploaded video when it is not playing. You can change this image to a different thumbnail by accessing the Edit Video screen and selecting from a set of thumbnails taken from still frames from your video. After you have set a thumbnail for your video, the image then appears on your friends' news feeds.

Set a Video Thumbnail

1 Click **Edit** on a video you have uploaded to Facebook.

The Edit Video screen appears.

2 Click the arrows to select a thumbnail image.

3 Click **Save**.

Listen to Music on Facebook

You can listen to music on Facebook after you have installed the required apps. Spotify is one of the most popular music apps on Facebook and allows you to share the music you are listening to with your friends and vice versa. Music that a friend listens to through an app or website can be sent to Facebook where you can choose to listen to the same music or playlist.

Listen to Music on Facebook

1 Click the **Play** button next to the activity of a friend.

Note: If you do not have the required app installed, Facebook prompts you to install it and set privacy settings.

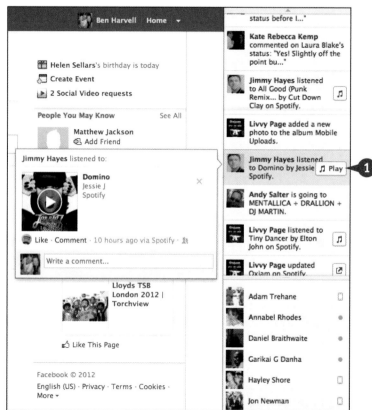

A message window appears.

 Click the button to open the app of the player associated with the music you clicked.

The app or website opens and your music begins playing.

Listen to Music with Friends

When a friend is listening to music with privacy controls set to share activity from a music app, you can see what he or she is listening to on your news feed. By clicking the **Listen** link below the story on your news feed, you can listen to the same song, album, or playlist using the same music app your friend uses. If you do not have the app installed or the correct software on your computer, Facebook asks to install the app or install and launch the software before you can listen to the music.

Listen to Music with Friends

 Click **Listen** beneath a story about a friend listening to music.

Facebook attempts to launch the required music application.

Note: If you do not have the required music app installed or running, Facebook asks you to install it or launch it.

The music your friend is listening to starts playing through the app.

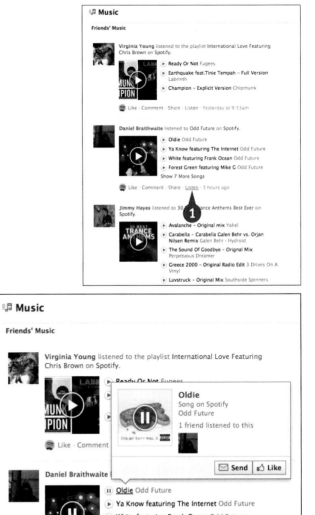

CHAPTER 10

Using Apps

Apps extend your Facebook experience, enabling you to play games, share your interests, and connect with like-minded fans of sports, books, and other entertainment. Discover how to add apps to your Timeline, buy Facebook credits, and block apps from accessing your account.

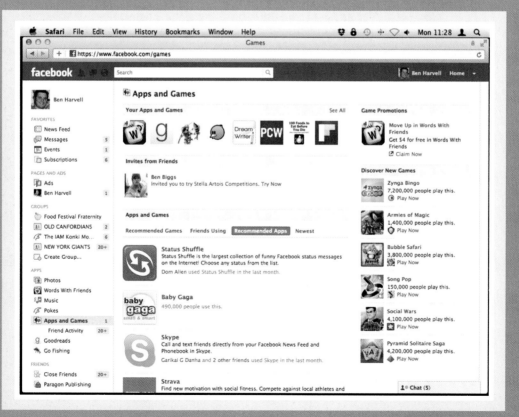

Find Apps

You can quickly find a wide range of apps on Facebook by clicking Apps and Games from the left column. The Apps and Games page lists new and featured apps and games as well as games and apps your friends are using. Apps can be installed from this page, and you can also view the apps you have installed already.

Find Apps

1 Click **Home**.

2 Click **Apps and Games**.

The Apps and Games screen appears.

A Your apps are shown at the top of the page.

B Click **See All** to show your installed apps.

C Click **Friend Activity** to see apps and games friends have used recently.

3 Click **Recommended Apps**.

A list of recommended apps and the friends using them appears.

④ Click the name of a recommended app.

The app info and install page appears.

How do I change the games listed in Discover New Games?

These are promoted games that you can remove in the same way as adverts. Simply position your mouse pointer over the game listing and click the X that appears.

How do I find out more about a recommended app?

The best method is to find the fan page for the app. On your home page, search for the app using the Search box at the top of the screen and look for a page related to it. Click the page to view more information on the app.

Install an App

You can install a variety of apps on Facebook that enable you to play games, share media, read articles, and many other options. Some apps use your profile information to create recommendations for you, and others post updates to your timeline. Installing an app often takes fewer than two clicks. Your installed apps are listed on the left column of your Facebook home page for quick access.

Install an App

1 Click the name of an app on Facebook.

The app installation screen appears.

Ⓐ Set who can see posts that this app makes on your behalf using the **Audience Selector** (👥 Friends).

Ⓑ Information the app gathers from your profile appears here.

2 Click **Go to App**.

Note: Games show **Play Game** and some apps may show **Allow**.

The app loads or takes you through a setup process.

 Click **Home**.

Ⓒ To access your app in future, click its name under the Apps section on the left column.

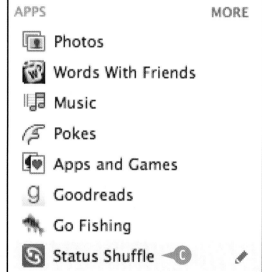

Why is an app asking for permission to access my information?

This differs between apps but is normally required to complete the setup or login process for an app. Other apps may want to access your information to create recommendations based on your likes and updates.

Does Facebook make all the apps I see?

No. Facebook does have its own apps, but most applications are made by developers and game companies for use on Facebook.

Add Apps to Your Timeline

A number of apps on Facebook are designed specifically to work with your Facebook timeline. These apps automatically add your activity, high scores in games, and other information, such as run tracking and check-ins, in their own space. Facebook provides a page to showcase timeline apps, and you can install most apps from that page. Timeline apps can be hidden, removed, and highlighted in the same way as other items on your timeline.

Add Apps to Your Timeline

1 Type **www.facebook.com/ about/timeline/apps** into the URL bar of your browser and press Enter (Return).

The Timeline Apps page appears.

2 Click a category.

3 Click the arrows to move between app pages.

4 Click the app you want to add to your timeline.

The app install page appears.

Note: Some apps may refer you to their home page, in which case you must search for the app page on Facebook or log in to Facebook through the site.

 Click **Go to App** or **Play Game**.

Facebook shows updates from the app on your timeline activity and in their own area.

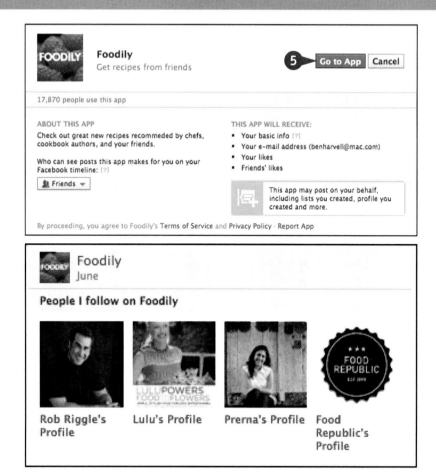

TIPS

What do apps do on my timeline?
Apps update in near to real time on your timeline and can post high scores from games, songs you listen to, articles you read, and more.

Who can see updates from timeline apps I install?
You can set who sees app updates on your timeline after it has been installed by using the **Audience Selector** (🔲 Friends) or the Ads, Apps and Websites page on the Privacy Settings screen.

Control App Information Shared with Friends

If your Facebook friends have access to information from your profile, the apps they use can also access this information in order to enhance the features the apps offer. This information can be profile data such as your birthday or relationships, or videos and photos you have shared, depending on the type of app being used. From the Apps, Games and Websites section of the Privacy Settings screen, you can set what information the apps that your friends use can access.

Control App Information Shared with Friends

1 Click the **Account** menu (▾).

2 Click **Privacy Settings**.

3 Click **Edit Settings** in the Ads, Apps and Websites section.

The Apps, Games and Websites privacy settings appear.

4 Click **Edit Settings**.

5 Uncheck any categories of information you do not want shared with your friends' apps (◉ changes to ◯).

6 Click **Save Changes**.

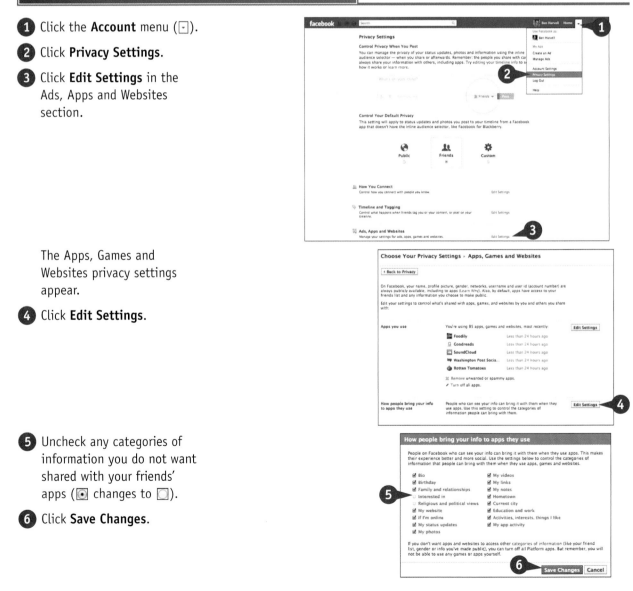

Remove Apps

You can use the Apps page on Facebook to remove any app you have installed. Removing an app deletes it from your timeline so that you can no longer access its features. Removed apps also no longer post updates on your timeline or appear in your recent activity updates. Once an app has been removed, you can install it again if you want.

Remove Apps

① Click **Home**.

② Click **Apps**.

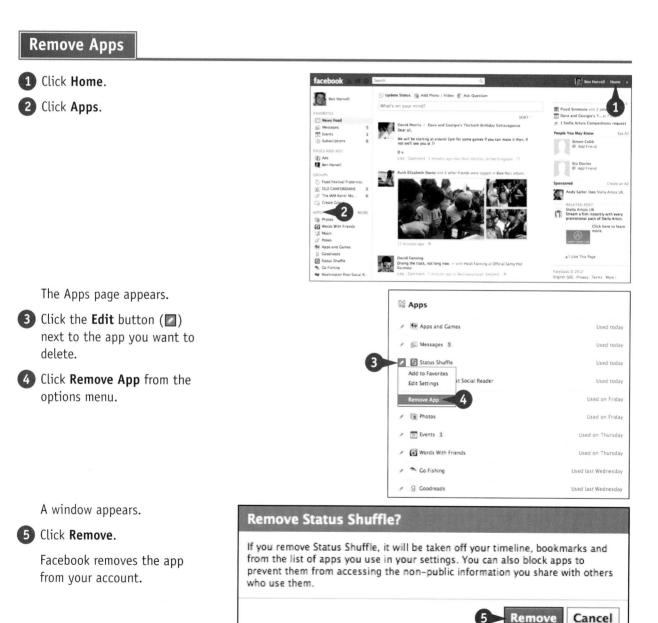

The Apps page appears.

③ Click the **Edit** button (▱) next to the app you want to delete.

④ Click **Remove App** from the options menu.

A window appears.

⑤ Click **Remove**.

Facebook removes the app from your account.

Add Bank Account Details

In order to buy Facebook Credits within apps on Facebook, you must add bank account details to your account information. You can do this from the Payments Settings screen under Account Settings. When you have added bank details to your account, the card details you add to your account is used when you buy Facebook Credits through apps and games on Facebook.

Add Bank Account Details

1 Click the **Account** menu ([-]).

2 Click **Account Settings** from the options menu.

3 Click **Payments**.

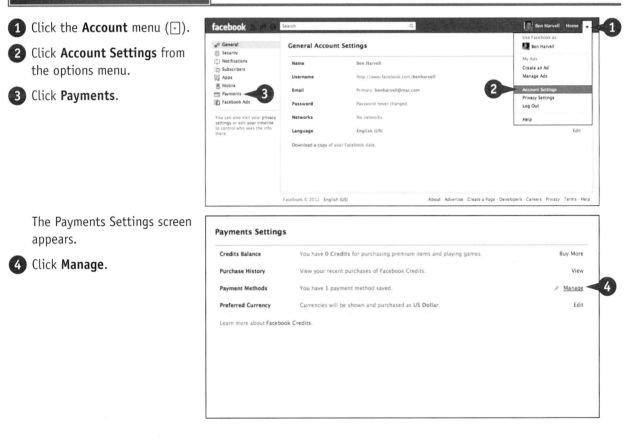

The Payments Settings screen appears.

4 Click **Manage**.

You are prompted to enter your password.

5 Type your password into the field.

6 Click **Continue**.

The Payment Methods section appears.

7 Type your bank details into the provided fields.

8 Click the arrow ([⬦]) and select your country from the drop-down menu.

9 Click **Add**.

Facebook saves your payment method.

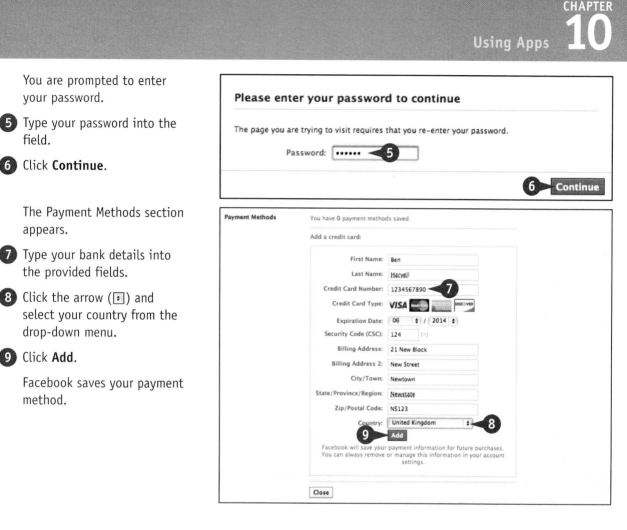

Do I have to add my credit card details?
You do not have to add card details to your Facebook account to use Facebook, only to make a purchase of Facebook Credits to use with an app.

Is it safe to add my bank account details?
Facebook uses a number of security measures to protect your details, including using secured servers, firewalls, and encryption. Facebook monitors your account to prevent identity theft and fraud, and never shares your financial information with third parties.

Buy Facebook Credits

Instead of making you pay cash directly, Facebook Credits offer a secure way to spend money within Facebook apps for purchasing upgrades in games and accessing advanced features. When you make a purchase within an app, Facebook asks you to provide bank details or select an account you already have on file. Facebook handles the payment through the credit card you have linked to your account and processes the payment securely.

Buy Facebook Credits

1 Within an app that uses Facebook credits, click **Buy**.

Note: Some apps may use different wording, such as Purchase.

Purchasing information for the app appears.

2 Make your selection and click **Continue**.

A payment window appears.

③ Select your payment method
(□ changes to ◉).

Ⓐ For more choices, click **More
Payment Options**.

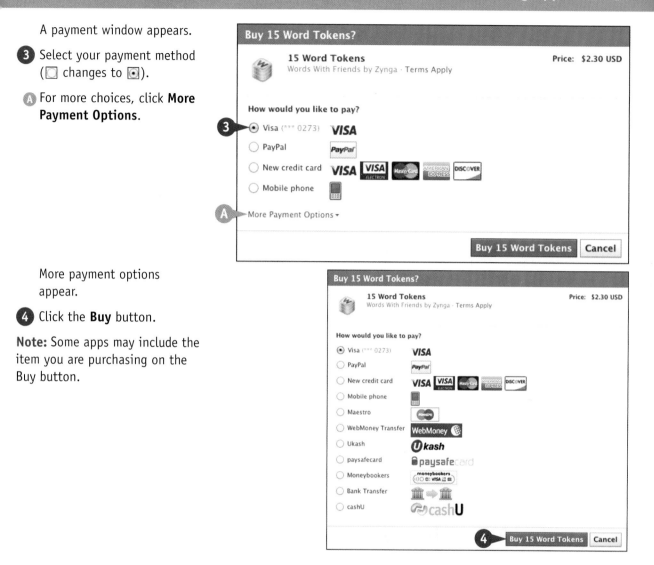

More payment options
appear.

④ Click the **Buy** button.

Note: Some apps may include the
item you are purchasing on the
Buy button.

TIPS

What is the Mobile Phone option on the payment screen?
You can pay for credits using your mobile phone if you have one linked to your Facebook account. The cost is added to your phone bill.

Can I use a different card from the one I have on file?
Yes. Select the **New credit card** option when you select your payment method and enter new card details.

Block an App

Blocking an app prevents it from accessing any information from your Facebook account and also prevents friends from sending you invitations or requests for the app. It also means that you will not see the app on Facebook even when friends install it. You can unblock an app at any time by visiting the Privacy Settings page and using the Manage Blocking section. When you unblock an app, you must grant it permission to access your account again if you want to use the app.

Block an App

① Locate or search for the Facebook page for the app you want to block.

② Click the **Action menu** button ().

③ Click **Block App** from the options menu.

The Block App? window appears.

④ Click **Okay**.

Block App?

Blocking Chill will prevent others from sending you invitations and requests for this app and will prevent this app from getting any info about you. This will also prevent you from seeing Chill if other people have it installed.

④  Okay   Cancel

Use Facebook Social Plugins on External Sites

You can use your Facebook account to log in to websites and online services instead of creating an account. This is most commonly found when commenting on articles on the web. Websites that use the Facebook social plugin allow you to log in with your Facebook account and send your comment or other information to your Facebook account if you want. If you are already logged in to Facebook, you may not have to sign in at all.

Use Facebook Social Plugins on External Sites

1 Locate the Facebook social plugin on a web page and type your comment if required.

2 Click **Comment using**.

3 Click **Facebook** from the options menu.

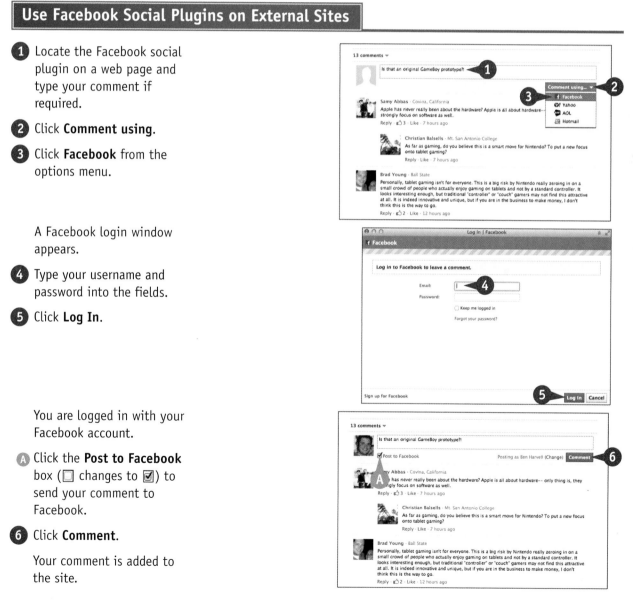

A Facebook login window appears.

4 Type your username and password into the fields.

5 Click **Log In**.

You are logged in with your Facebook account.

Ⓐ Click the **Post to Facebook** box (☐ changes to ☑) to send your comment to Facebook.

6 Click **Comment**.

Your comment is added to the site.

Use Instant Personalization on External Sites

You can use Facebook on external websites compatible with instant personalization to see recommendations from friends and share your activity. Facebook has collaborated with a handful of websites, including TripAdvisor, Bing, and Rotten Tomatoes, to provide you with a more social experience when visiting these sites. Instant personalization automatically shows comments and reviews your friends have posted to the website, and allows you to post information from the site to Facebook.

Use Instant Personalization on External Sites

1 Log in to Facebook.

2 Type **www.facebook.com/instantpersonalization/** into the URL bar of your browser and press **Enter** (**Return**).

The Instant Personalization page appears.

3 Click a partner site on which you want to use instant personalization.

The partner site loads and uses your Facebook data to log you in and show information from your friends.

196

Turn Off Apps

You can turn off Facebook apps to prevent them from connecting with your friends or accessing your information. Unlike removing or blocking an app, turning off an app allows you to continue using it, but you may lose some information and settings. You can turn an app back on at any time by visiting the Privacy Settings page for apps, games, and websites under Account Settings.

Turn Off Apps

1 Click the **Account** menu ([·]).

2 Click **Privacy Settings** from the options menu.

3 Click **Edit Settings** in the Ads, Apps and Websites section.

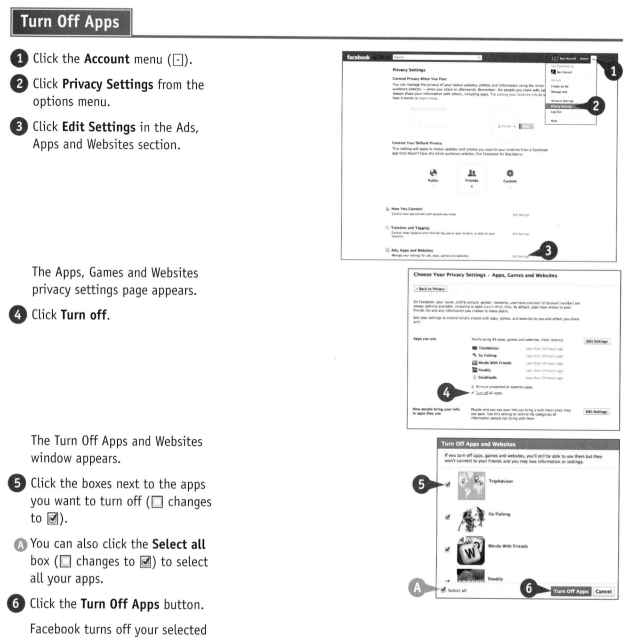

The Apps, Games and Websites privacy settings page appears.

4 Click **Turn off**.

The Turn Off Apps and Websites window appears.

5 Click the boxes next to the apps you want to turn off (☐ changes to ☑).

Ⓐ You can also click the **Select all** box (☐ changes to ☑) to select all your apps.

6 Click the **Turn Off Apps** button.

Facebook turns off your selected apps.

CHAPTER 11

Working with Notes

Using Facebook Notes, you can create longer, blog-style posts complete with images and text formatting to share with Friends. Notes can be tagged with the names of friends, and friends can add comments to your notes or share them with other friends.

Create a Note

You can write longer Facebook updates or blog-style posts on Facebook using the Notes feature. Notes offers a simple text-editing interface within which you can write as much text as you want, complete with a title and image attachments. You can preview your note before you save it, and it will appear on your timeline and on the news feeds of your friends after you publish it.

Create a Note

1 Click **Home**.

2 Click **Notes** under Apps from the left column.

Note: You may need to click **Apps** to show the Notes app.

The Notes screen appears.

3 Click **Write a Note**.

The Write a Note interface appears.

4 Type the title of your note into the **Title** field.

5 Type your note into the **Body** field.

A Click **Save Draft** to return to your note later.

B Click **Discard** to delete the current note.

6 Click **Publish**.

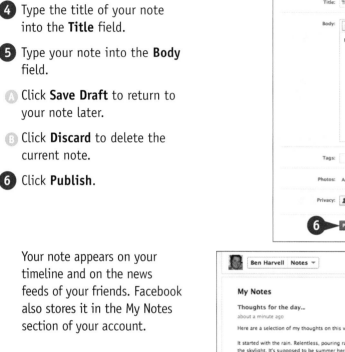

Your note appears on your timeline and on the news feeds of your friends. Facebook also stores it in the My Notes section of your account.

View Notes

The Notes screen shows all notes posted by your friends in compact view with only the initial text included. From this view you can like and comment on each note. Clicking View Full Note takes you to the complete note. From the Notes screen you can also view more posts from a specific friend by clicking More from.

View Notes

1 Click **Home**.

2 Click **Notes**.

Note: You may need to click **Apps** to show the Notes app.

The Notes screen appears.

3 Click **View Full Note** to show the whole note.

A You can also click **More from** to show more from the poster of the note.

Tag Notes

You can tag notes with the names of friends before you publish so that they are notified and others see their involvement with the tag. You can tag as many friends as you want in a note by typing their name into the Tags field within the Notes interface. Tagged friends receive a notification when they are tagged in a note, and other friends can also see the tags when they view the note.

Tag Notes

1 Click **Home**.

2 Click **Notes**.

3 Click **Write a Note**.

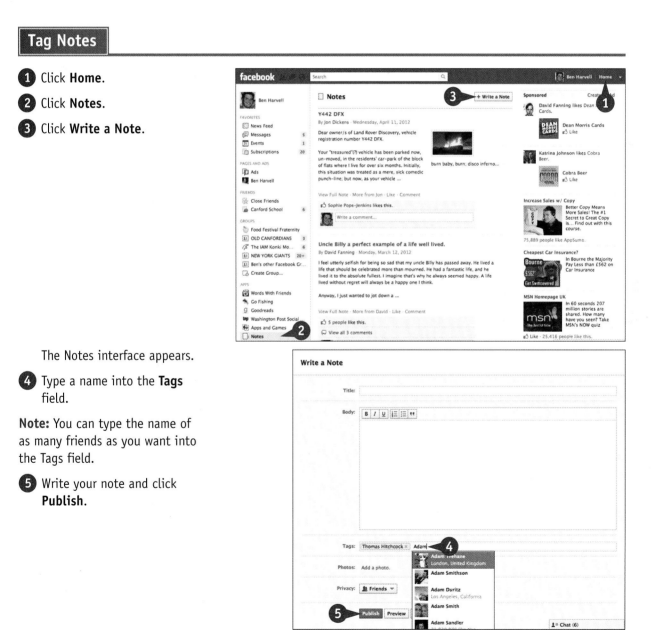

The Notes interface appears.

4 Type a name into the **Tags** field.

Note: You can type the name of as many friends as you want into the Tags field.

5 Write your note and click **Publish**.

View Draft Notes

You can view drafts of Notes you have started but not completed on the My Drafts screen. This screen shows all Notes that you have written but not published or discarded and the date and time they were last edited. From the My Drafts screen you can permanently delete drafts or edit them and publish them. None of your friends can see your draft Notes until you publish them.

View Draft Notes

1 Click **Home**.

2 Click **Notes**.

3 Click **My Drafts**.

The My Drafts screen appears.

Ⓐ Click the title of a draft to view its content.

Ⓑ Click **Edit** to adjust the content of a draft.

Ⓒ Click **Discard** to delete a draft note.

View Notes About You

The Notes About Me screen shows all the notes in which friends have tagged you. Friends can tag a note to highlight the fact that you are mentioned in the note or to bring the note to your attention. You can view notes in which you have been tagged on this page and add comments to the notes or click to view the entire note.

View Notes About You

1 Click **Home**.

2 Click **Notes**.

3 Click **Notes About Me**.

The Notes About Me screen appears.

A Click the title of a note in which you are tagged.

B Type into the **Write a comment** field to comment on a note in which you are tagged.

Add a Photo to a Note

hotos can be uploaded to Facebook and added to notes you write. You can upload a selection of images to add to a note and position them using the layout buttons on the Write a Note interface. You can also add a caption to each image that you add to a note to provide a description of the photo you have included.

Add a Photo to a Note

1 On the Write a Note interface, click **Add a photo**.

Write a Note

Title:

Body: B / U ≣ ≣ tt

Tags:

Photos: Add a photo. **1**

Privacy: 👥 Friends ▾

Publish   Preview   Save Draft   Discard

2 Click **Choose File**.

Write a Note

Title:

Body: B / U ≣ ≣ tt

Tags:

Photos: No photos.

Upload a Photo

2 Choose File   no file selected

A file browser window appears.

③ Select the photo you want to add to your note.

④ Click **Choose**.

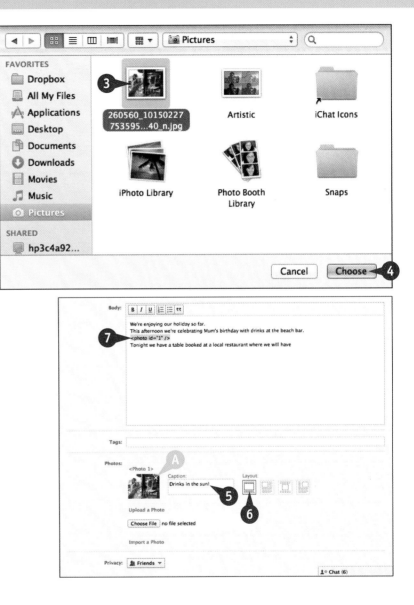

⑤ Type a caption into the **Caption** field.

⑥ Click one of the layout options to set the position of your image.

⑦ Copy and paste the image code to a location within your text.

Ⓐ To remove a photo from your note, click the X.

TIP

How do the layout buttons affect my note?
The layout buttons set how your image sits within the text of your note. You can choose to have an image appear at a large size between lines of text, aligned at a smaller size to the top left, centered at a smaller size, or aligned to the top right at a smaller size. You can adjust the layout of an image using these buttons at any time during the editing of a note and see how the image will look by clicking **Preview**.

You can preview a note before you make it public on Facebook. After you have created a note or opened a draft note, you can click the **Preview** button to launch the preview interface. The preview of your note shows you how it will appear after it is published and enables you to spot errors and determine the best position for images. You can publish your note directly from the preview screen or return to the Write a Note interface for further editing.

Preview a Note

1 With a new or draft note open, click **Preview**.

A preview of your note appears.

A To continue editing your note, click **Edit**.

B To publish your note, click **Publish**.

Edit a Note

You can make changes to a note that you have already published by viewing it while logged in to your Facebook account and clicking **Edit**. Clicking **Edit** returns you to the Write a Note interface where you can make changes to the text, tags, formatting, and images in the note, and the audience it is shared with. You can also choose to delete a note from the editing screen by clicking **Delete**. This permanently removes the note from Facebook.

Edit a Note

1 Click the title of a note you have published.

2 Click **Edit**.

3 Make changes to your note text.

Ⓐ You can also add a photo to an existing note by clicking **Add a photo.**

4 Click **Save**.

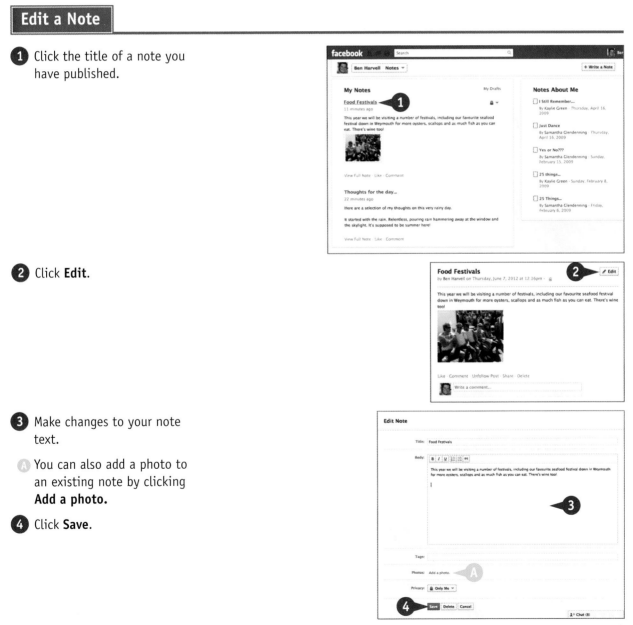

Set Note Privacy

You can set who can see your note by using the Audience Selector on the Write a Note or Edit Note screen and also on the My Notes screen. The Audience Selector button appears above the Save, Delete, and Cancel buttons within the Notes interface. On the My Notes screen you can quickly set the audience for your notes without having to view the full note by accessing the smaller Audience Selector that appears next to each note title.

Set Note Privacy

1 Click **Home**.

2 Click **Notes**.

3 Click **My Notes**.

A list of your published notes appears.

4 Click the **Audience Selector** (▣▾) next to a note title.

5 From the options menu, click the group you want to allow to see the note.

Apply Formatting to a Note

You can change the way text looks in a note by using the format buttons at the top of the Write a Note interface. Using these buttons you can make text bold, italic, or underlined. You can also create lists using numbers or bullet points and use the quotation button to show text as a quote that stands out from your body text. When you click a formatting button, Facebook adds HTML code to the note to apply the format you have chosen. You are free to copy and paste or enter your own HTML code if you want to. For example, you could enclose a word with the opening tag **<b>** and the closing tag **</b>** to make it bold.

Apply Formatting to a Note

1 Click the title of a draft note or a note you have published.

2 Click **Edit**.

The Edit Note interface appears.

3 Select a section of text in the Body field.

A Click the **B** button to make the text bold.

B Click the **I** button to make the text italic.

C Click the **U** button to underline the text.

D Click the **Numbered List** button to create a numbered list.

E Click the **Bulleted List** button to create a list of bullet points.

F Click the **Quotation Marks** button to quote text.

4 Click **Save**.

Food Festivals
by Ben Harvell on Thursday, June 7, 2012 at 12:16pm ·

✏ Edit

This year we will be visiting a number of festivals, including our favourite seafood festival down in Weymouth for more oysters, scallops and as much fish as you can eat. There's wine too!

Like · Comment · Unfollow Post · Share · Delete

Write a comment...

Edit Note

Title:

Body: B I U ☰ ☰ ❝

This year we will be visiting a number of festivals, including our favourite seafood festival down in Weymouth... and as much fish as you can eat. There's wine too!

Tags:

Photos: Add a photo.

Privacy: 🔒 Only Me ▾

Save Delete Cancel

Comment on a Note

You can comment on notes in the same way as any other story on Facebook. The comments space appears below the preview of a note and on the main page for the note. You can also like a note or like any of the comments made on the note. When you comment on a note, Facebook notifies the friend who wrote it of your comment. Facebook also notifies your friend if you like a note he or she has published.

Comment on a Note

1 Click **Home**.

2 Click **Notes**.

3 Type your comment into the **Write a comment** field and press Enter (Return).

Facebook adds your comment.

A You can also like a note by clicking **Like** below it.

ou can share a note to your own timeline, on the timeline of a friend, to a group, or to a page by clicking **Share** below a note. You can also share a note as a private message on Facebook. When you share a note, you can add your own comment so that others can see your thoughts on it.

Share a Note

1 Click **Share** below a note.

Food Festivals ✏ Edit
by Ben Harvell on Thursday, June 7, 2012 at 12:16pm · 🔒

This year we will be visiting a number of festivals, including our favourite seafood festival down in Weymouth for more oysters, scallops and as much fish as you can eat. There's wine too!

Like · Comment · Unfollow Post · Share · Delete

Write a comment...

The Share This Note window appears.

2 Click **On your own timeline**.

3 Select whom to share the note with from the options menu.

4 Type a comment on the note into the **Write Something** field.

5 Click **Share Note**.

Facebook shares the note to the location you selected.

Share this Note

Share: On your own timeline ▼ — 2 👥 Friends ▼

✓ On your own timeline
On a friend's timeline — 3
In a group
On your Page
In a private Message

Food
By Ben
This year we will be visiting a number of festivals, including our favourite seafood festival down in Weymouth for more oysters, scallops and as much fish as you can eat. There's wine too!

5 → **Share Note** Cancel

CHAPTER 12

Using Search and Notifications

Use the Facebook search tool to find friends and other content like pages or groups, or to access specific sections of Facebook quickly. Set your Facebook notifications so you are alerted when certain events occur on Facebook, such as photo tagging or messages.

Search for People and Content

You can search for people, apps, and pages using the Search box at the top of the Facebook interface. Facebook analyzes your search criteria and provides results that it believes are most relevant to you at the top of the *typeahead*, which is the menu that appears as you search. To view more search results, you can click the **See More Search Results** option to show a page of results for your search.

Search for People and Content

1 Click **Home**.

2 Type your search into the Search box.

A Results Facebook determines are relevant to you appear first on the typeahead.

B Search results are split into People, Pages, and Apps.

3 Click **See more results**.

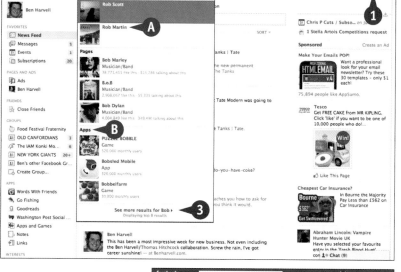

Facebook shows all results for your search.

C To view more results, click **See More Results**.

D Results from the web are shown below the Facebook search results.

Filter Search Results

Y ou can filter your search results on Facebook by People, Pages, Places, Groups, and more using the Search Filters column at the left of the search results page. By default, the search results page shows the most relevant results from all areas of Facebook, but when using filters, only a specific type of content is shown. You can also search for content from the web and in posts using filters.

Filter Search Results

1 Click **Home**.

2 Type your search into the Search box.

3 Click **See more results**.

The results page appears.

4 Click a filter from the left column.

Facebook filters the results to show only the type of content you selected.

Find Friends Through Search

You can use the Facebook search feature to look for friends who might be on Facebook but have not been added as a friend. Using the search filters to show only people in the search results, as well as further filters to streamline your search to show people by education, location, or workplace, you can quickly narrow down your search to find the person you are looking for. You can then view how many friends you have in common with that person and send him or her a message or add the person as a friend.

Find Friends Through Search

1. Click **Home**.

2. Type a name into the Search box.

   A. If the person you are looking for appears in the drop-down menu, click the result to view his or her profile.

3. Click **See more results**.

   The results page appears.

4. Click **People**.

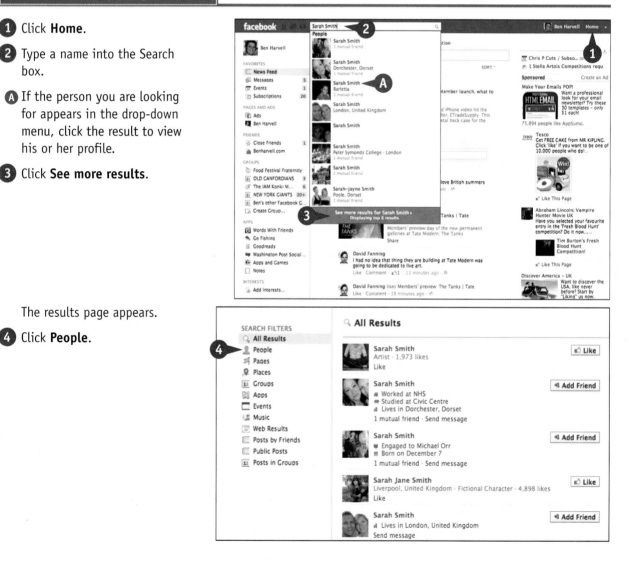

Facebook filters the results to show only people.

 Click the **Location** button and select Location, Education, or Workplace from the options menu.

 Type a city, school, or company into the field and press [Enter] ([Return]).

People

SEARCH TOOLS

Location ▾   Type the name of a city or region.

✓ Location

Education

Workplace

RESULTS

Sarah Smith   Add Friend
• Worked at NHS
• Studied at Civic Centre
• Lives in Dorchester, Dorset
1 mutual friend · Send message

Sarah Smith   Add Friend
• Engaged to Michael Orr
• Born on December 7
1 mutual friend · Send message

Sarah Smith   Add Friend
• Lives in London, United Kingdom
Send message

Sarah Smith   Add Friend
• Lives in London, United Kingdom
• From Bournemouth
• Born on August 8, 1984
1 mutual friend · Send message

The results are filtered further.

Ⓑ Click **Add another filter...** to further filter your results.

 Click the name of a person to view their profile.

People

SEARCH TOOLS

Location ▾   Sydney, NSW
Add another filter...

RESULTS

Sarah Smith   Add Friend
• Worked at Part Time Sales Assistant
• Lives in Sydney, Australia
• It's complicated
Send message

Sarah Smith   Add Friend
• Worked at Tiffanys girls
• Went to Riverside Girls High School
• Lives in Sydney, Australia
Send message

Sarah Smith   Add Friend
• Worked at not yet
• Studied at The Australian National University
• Lives in Sydney, Australia
Send message

Sarah Smith   Add Friend
• Lives in Sydney, Australia
Send message

Sarah Smith   Add Friend
• Lives in Sydney, Australia
Send message

Sarah Smith   Add Friend
• Lives in Sydney, Australia
Send message

Sarah Smith   Add Friend
• Lives in Sydney, Australia
• From Stockholm, Sweden
Send message

TIP

How do I know if I have found the person I am looking for?
Below the people listed in the search results is information such as where they work, where they live, and how many friends you have in common with them. You can also position the mouse cursor over the name of a person to see a larger profile picture as well as the profile pictures of mutual friends. Anyone who has restricted the information they share will appear with a generic placeholder image when they appear in a search. If you still cannot determine if you have found the person you are looking for, you can click their name to view their public profile or send them a message by clicking **Send Message**.

Search for Friends on Chat

If you have many friends on Facebook, you cannot see all of them on the Chat list at one time. To quickly find friends to chat with, you can use the Search box that appears at the bottom of the chat interface. As you type, the list of available friends shrinks until you find the person you want to chat with.

Search for Friends on Chat

1 Expand the chat interface by clicking **Chat** at the bottom right of the interface.

Note: If your browser is set to a larger width, the chat interface may already be visible.

2 Click the Search box and type the name of a friend on Facebook.

The Chat list reduces to show only names that match your search criteria.

Facebook filters the results to show only people.

5 Click the **Location** button and select Location, Education, or Workplace from the options menu.

6 Type a city, school, or company into the field and press Enter (Return).

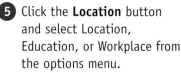

The results are filtered further.

B Click **Add another filter...** to further filter your results.

7 Click the name of a person to view their profile.

TIP

How do I know if I have found the person I am looking for?
Below the people listed in the search results is information such as where they work, where they live, and how many friends you have in common with them. You can also position the mouse cursor over the name of a person to see a larger profile picture as well as the profile pictures of mutual friends. Anyone who has restricted the information they share will appear with a generic placeholder image when they appear in a search. If you still cannot determine if you have found the person you are looking for, you can click their name to view their public profile or send them a message by clicking **Send Message**.

Search for Friends on Chat

If you have many friends on Facebook, you cannot see all of them on the Chat list at one time. To quickly find friends to chat with, you can use the Search box that appears at the bottom of the chat interface. As you type, the list of available friends shrinks until you find the person you want to chat with.

Search for Friends on Chat

① Expand the chat interface by clicking **Chat** at the bottom right of the interface.

Note: If your browser is set to a larger width, the chat interface may already be visible.

② Click the Search box and type the name of a friend on Facebook.

The Chat list reduces to show only names that match your search criteria.

View Recent Notifications

From the Notifications section of the Account Settings screen, you can view notifications that Facebook has sent you. From here you can view the notifications you receive most often and toggle the type of notification to your liking. Recent Notifications are shown in chronological order and divided into groups by day and the past week. You can also use the **See More** link to show more notifications from the past week if you want.

View Recent Notifications

1 Click **Home**.

2 Click the **Account** menu (▾).

3 Click **Account Settings** from the options menu.

4 Click **Notifications**.

The Notifications Settings screen appears.

Ⓐ Click a link to view a person or other content about which you have been notified.

Ⓑ Click the envelope button next to a notification to toggle that notification type on or off.

Ⓒ Click **See More** to view more Recent Notifications.

Set Facebook Notifications

You can set what activity Facebook notifies you about from the Notifications Settings screen. These notifications include messages sent to you on Facebook, people adding you as a friend, friend confirmations, and tags. You can set custom notification settings by toggling individual notifications on or off, or you can choose to turn all notifications on or off. These changes are saved on the Notifications Settings screen and can be edited at any time.

Set Facebook Notifications

1 Click **Home**.

2 Click the **Account** menu (⊡).

3 Click **Account Settings** from the options menu.

4 Click **Notifications**.

5 Click **Facebook**.

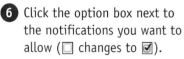

A list of Facebook notifications appears.

Note: You may need to scroll back to the All Notifications section if your browser refreshes.

6 Click the option box next to the notifications you want to allow (☐ changes to ☑).

A Click the envelope button to select or deselect all notifications.

7 Click **Save Changes**.

222

Set App Notifications

From the Notifications screen under Account Settings, you can set which applications on Facebook have permission to send you e-mail messages. Applications cannot send messages to the e-mail account you have linked to Facebook if you turn off notifications for them. You can select specific apps to allow to send you e-mail, or you can toggle permission on and off for all the apps you use on Facebook.

Set App Notifications

1 Click **Home**.

2 Click the **Account** menu ([·]).

3 Click **Account Settings** from the options menu.

4 Click **Notifications**.

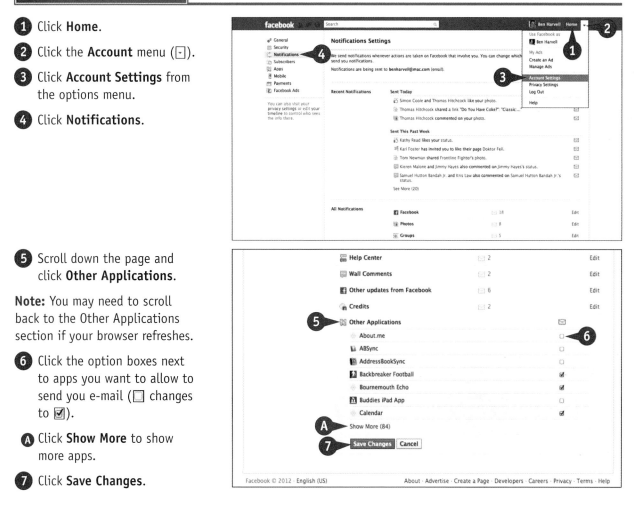

5 Scroll down the page and click **Other Applications**.

Note: You may need to scroll back to the Other Applications section if your browser refreshes.

6 Click the option boxes next to apps you want to allow to send you e-mail (☐ changes to ☑).

A Click **Show More** to show more apps.

7 Click **Save Changes**.

Set Photo Notifications

By default you are sent notifications when you are tagged in a photo, when someone tags one of your photos, or when comments are made on one of your photos or a photo of you. You can toggle these notifications, as well as other photo-related notifications, on or off using the Notifications Settings screen. By checking individual boxes, you can customize the actions that trigger a notification and reduce the number of alerts you receive from Facebook.

Set Photo Notifications

1 Click **Home**.

2 Click the **Account** menu (⊡).

3 Click **Account Settings** from the options menu.

4 Click **Notifications**.

5 Click **Edit**.

Note: You may need to scroll back to the Photos section if your browser refreshes.

6 Click the option boxes next to the actions you want to be notified about (☐ changes to ☑).

7 Click **Save Changes**.

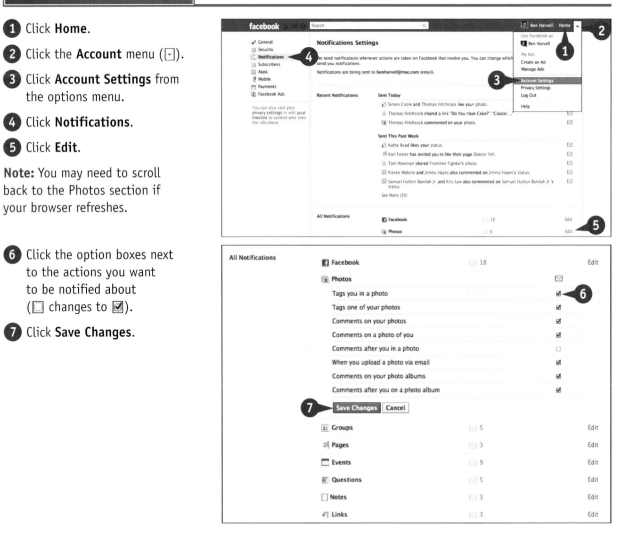

Set List Notifications

By default, lists you create on Facebook send you notifications when those within the list make changes to their account, upload photos, and make comments. By adjusting the type of notifications you receive from Facebook lists, you can limit the number of alerts you receive via e-mail or on Facebook or turn them off completely. The notification level can be set using the **Notifications** button found at the top right of the List page.

Set List Notifications

① Click the name of a list from the left column.

② Click **Notifications**.

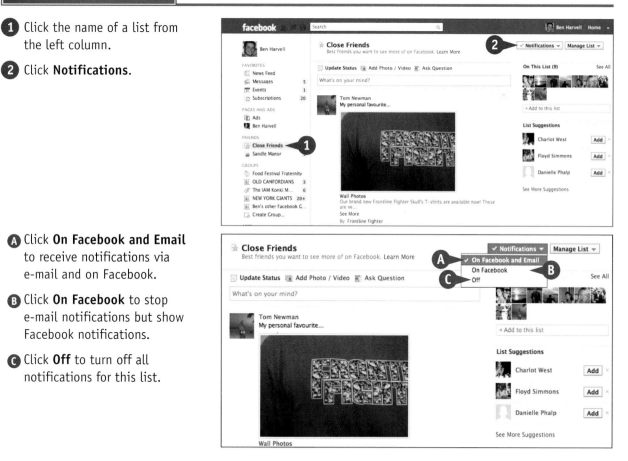

Ⓐ Click **On Facebook and Email** to receive notifications via e-mail and on Facebook.

Ⓑ Click **On Facebook** to stop e-mail notifications but show Facebook notifications.

Ⓒ Click **Off** to turn off all notifications for this list.

Set Event Notifications

You can adjust the level of notifications you receive from events you have been invited to or are attending on Facebook. Often, events with a large number of invitees can produce an unwanted level of notifications as people write on the wall or add comments to the event. You can turn all notifications for an event off or select a custom level of notifications, such as when you are invited to an event and when the event time and date is changed or if it is cancelled.

Set Event Notifications

1 Click **Home**.

2 Click the **Account** menu (⊡).

3 Click **Account Settings** from the options menu.

4 Click **Notifications**.

5 Click **Edit**.

Note: You may need to scroll back to the Events section if your browser refreshes.

6 Click the option boxes next to the actions you want to be notified about (☐ changes to ☑).

7 Click **Save Changes**.

Set Individual Group E-Mail Notifications

You can set custom notification levels for groups on Facebook using the Notifications Settings screen. This includes changes to the name of a group, invitations to a group, and adjustments to the privacy settings of a group. You can also set which specific groups trigger e-mail notifications and which do not. You can only adjust group e-mail settings for groups of which you are a member.

Set Individual Group E-Mail Notifications

 1 Click **Home**.

2 Click the **Account** menu (⊡).

3 Click **Account Settings** from the options menu.

4 Click **Notifications**.

5 Click **Edit**.

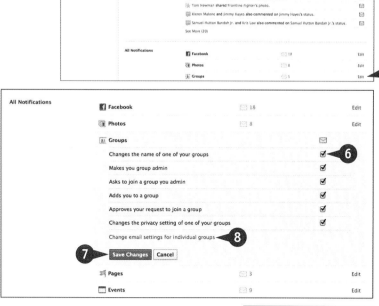

Note: You may need to scroll back to the Groups section if your browser refreshes.

6 Click the option boxes next to the actions you want to be notified about (☐ changes to ☑).

7 Click **Save Changes**.

8 Click **Change email settings for individual groups**.

The Group Email Settings window appears.

9 Click the option boxes next to the groups you want to be notified about by e-mail (☐ changes to ☑).

10 Click **Save**.

Search for Multiple Criteria

Rather than search for one term using Facebook Search, you can add a second term by splitting your search criteria into two parts, using a "pipe" which can be added by typing **Shift** and **** at the same time. By placing two search terms either side of this symbol, you can search for two elements at once to narrow down your search faster.

Search for Multiple Criteria

1 Type your first search term into the Search box.

2 Add a space and a "pipe" after your first search term by pressing **Shift** + **** .

3 Add another space and type your second search term.

4 Click **See more results**.

Results for both of your search terms appear.

Search Public Posts

Y ou can find posts on a given topic on Facebook from people outside your network by searching public posts using the search filters. The search results show any posts on Facebook that include the search terms you have selected and that other Facebook users have made public. This is a useful way to find out about a particular topic or find interesting people to subscribe to on Facebook.

Search Public Posts

1 Click **Home**.

2 Type your search into the Search box.

3 Click **See more results**.

The results page appears.

4 Click **Public Posts**.

A list of posts containing your search criteria that have been made public is shown.

CHAPTER 13

Accessing Facebook Mobile

You can use Facebook wherever you happen to be via your smartphone or tablet device. Facebook enables you to upload photos, set your status, and share your location with friends.

Introducing Facebook Mobile

You can access your Facebook account on your smartphone or tablet device if you have an Internet connection. Through the dedicated Facebook app, available for most smartphones, you can update your status, view updates from friends, and even share photos without having to access Facebook on your computer. By using Facebook on your mobile device, you can access most of the features found in Facebook on your computer, including apps, updates, and friend lists, and you can also receive notifications on your mobile device as you do when using Facebook on your computer. The level of security in Facebook mobile is also similar to that of the browser-based Facebook experience.

Installation and Setup

On smartphones and tablet devices, you must install the Facebook Mobile app via the app store or marketplace for your chosen device. Once you have downloaded the app to your device, you can sign in to your account using the same login details you use to access Facebook on your computer. Any changes you make to your Facebook account from your mobile device are reflected on your Facebook account on the web, although there may be a delay in seeing updates from the app if you are moving in and out of cellphone or Wi-Fi signal range with your device.

Updates and Uploads

When a network connection is available, you can update your status, comment on photos, send messages, and share photos from Facebook Mobile on your mobile device. You need a strong network connection using Edge, 3G, 4G, or, ideally, Wi-Fi to upload large photos or large batches of photos. Although you can upload videos, this may take longer, which can cause problems when using a mobile network or moving from place to place. When you upload content from a mobile device, you can use the Audience Selector to determine who can see that content and also select media from the photo library on your device.

Notifications

Depending on the settings you use with Facebook Mobile, you can receive notifications from the mobile app as you do when logged in to Facebook on your computer. These notifications appear not only within Facebook Mobile, but also as notifications on your mobile device that work in the same way as e-mail alerts or SMS messages. As with Facebook on your computer, you can tell Facebook Mobile which events to alert you about and which to ignore. This can be useful, for example, if you want to be alerted when you receive an incoming message on Facebook, but not when you are tagged in a photo or when friends update their status.

Check-ins and Location

If your mobile device includes built-in GPS or you are using a Wi-Fi hotspot, you can use Facebook Mobile to "check in" at locations you visit. GPS within your device is far more accurate than Wi-Fi, which includes a location based on the rough data provided by the Wi-Fi hotspot you are using. When you tap the Check In button within Facebook Mobile, the app attempts to locate you and suggest places you may want to check out. This can include restaurants, bars, and sporting events, and Facebook Mobile adds the information to your Facebook timeline. You can also use these location features to add a location to status updates as well as photos you upload from your mobile device.

Access Facebook Mobile on an iPhone

You can access Facebook on an iPhone in two ways. The first is via Safari using the Facebook mobile browser interface, and the second is by using the Facebook Mobile app. Both ways offer a similar set of features, but the mobile app offers the added benefit of notifications delivered through the app to your phone, even when you are not using it. Using Push notifications, however, does drain the battery more quickly on mobile devices. The Facebook mobile browser interface and the Facebook Mobile app require a connection to the Internet from your device to work correctly.

Access Facebook Mobile on an iPhone

Access Facebook via the Safari Browser

 Type **www.facebook.com** into the URL bar of the Safari browser.

2 Tap **Go**.

3 Type your Facebook e-mail address and password into the required fields.

4 Tap **Log In**.

Your Facebook account appears in the browser.

Access Facebook via the Facebook Mobile App

1 Tap the **Facebook** icon on your iPhone Home screen.

The Facebook app launches.

2 Type your e-mail address and password into the fields that appear.

3 Tap **Log In**.

Your Facebook account appears within the app.

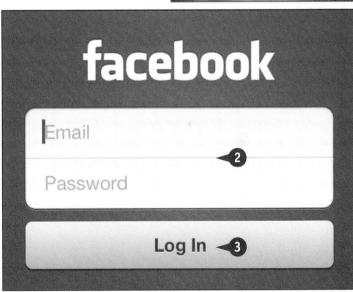

 TIP

Can I use the Chat and Messages features with mobile versions of Facebook?

Yes. You can access the Facebook Chat and Messages interfaces from the left pane of the Facebook mobile site and app. You can contact friends who are available to chat from the Chat screen, which allows you to type and receive messages. Messages looks similar to Messages on the desktop version of Facebook and lists all messages you have received. On an iPhone, you can also call or send an SMS message to friends who have included their contact details in their profile. Those who have included contact details have a small telephone symbol next to their name on the friends list.

Access Facebook Mobile on an iPad

The Facebook app for iPad is different from the iPhone version in a number of ways, including a different and larger layout. The web version differs slightly in terms of size but is similar to the iPhone version. The iPad version can also access the regular Facebook site, but some features that require Adobe Flash are not available. Both the iPhone and iPad can access the browser-based Facebook interface and use the Facebook app for iPhone and iPad. You must log in to your Facebook account when visiting both the mobile and app versions of Facebook.

Access Facebook Mobile on an iPad

Access Facebook via the Safari Browser

1 Type **www.facebook.com** into the URL bar of the Safari browser.

Note: You can also type **m.facebook.com** into the URL bar to load the mobile version of Facebook.

2 Tap **Go**.

3 Type your Facebook e-mail address and password into the required fields.

4 Tap **Log In**.

Your Facebook account appears in the browser.

Access Facebook via the Facebook iPad App

1 Tap the **Facebook** icon on your iPad Home screen.

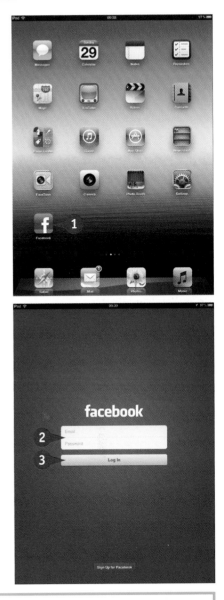

The Facebook app launches.

2 Type your e-mail address and password into the fields that appear.

3 Tap **Log In**.

Your Facebook account appears within the app.

TIPS

Can I use Facebook on my iPad without an Internet connection?
No, you cannot use the Facebook app for iPad or the mobile browser version of Facebook without an Internet connection. You may be able to access basic information from the iPad Facebook app when a connection is not present, but you cannot update your status or view new content. Both the app and browser-based versions of Facebook update when a connection to the Internet becomes available.

Can I upload photos using Facebook on my iPad?
You can upload photos from the Facebook app on an iPad but not from the browser-based version, as it requires Adobe Flash to work. The same applies for videos.

Access Facebook Mobile on Android

Connecting to Facebook via an Android device is similar to connecting with an iPhone, except for a few minor differences. A wide range of Android devices are available — this example uses an HTC smartphone. The process, however, is similar for all Android handsets, as they generally use the same software. The Facebook app is often preinstalled on Android handsets, and you can set it up the first time you use the phone or at a later time by launching the Facebook app.

Access Facebook Mobile on Android

Access the Facebook Mobile Site

1 Launch the Internet app on your device and type **www.facebook.com** into the URL bar.

2 Tap **Go**.

The Facebook mobile site loads.

3 Type your login details into the fields that appear.

4 Tap **Log in**.

The app logs you in to the Facebook mobile site.

Access the Facebook Mobile App

1 Tap the **Facebook** app icon on the home screen of your device.

The Facebook app launches.

2 Type your Facebook login details into the fields that appear.

3 Tap **Login**.

The app logs you in to your Facebook account.

Why do I see a message about sync options when I log in?

Some devices, such as those from HTC, offer a syncing service with Facebook that allows you to sync contacts between your account and your device. You can choose to use this feature or to turn it off completely.

Can I share photos from an Android device?

Yes. You can use the Facebook app on Android to share photos in the same way as you would on an iPhone or iPad. Tap the **Photo** button on your timeline or news feed, and select whether you want to take a photo to upload or select a photo already stored on your device.

The Facebook iPad app offers many of the features found in the desktop version of Facebook, including the ability to update your status. As long as you have an Internet connection, you can share an update as you would when using the regular Facebook platform, and it appears on your timeline and the news feeds of your friends.

Update Your Status via the Facebook iPad App

1 Swipe across the Facebook app interface from left to right.

The navigation pane appears.

2 Tap **News Feed**.

3 Tap **Status.**

4 Type a status message into the pop-up menu that appears using the on-screen keyboard.

A Tap the icons at the bottom of the pop-up menu to add people, locations, and photos to your update.

5 Tap **Audience Selector** ().

6 Tap the audience you want to be able to view your update.

 7 Tap **Post**.

Your update now appears on your news feed.

How can I view posts I have made with the Facebook app?
You can view your posts in two ways. First, you can view them on your profile page within the app by tapping the menu button at the top left of the app and tapping your name in the left pane. You can also view posts from yourself and others by tapping News Feed in the left pane.

How do I delete a status update I have made with the Facebook app?
You can delete posts from your news feed by swiping a finger across them from left to right. Tap the **Remove** button that appears to delete the post from Facebook.

Take and Upload Photos with the Facebook App

You can shoot photos and videos from within the Facebook app on your mobile device and upload them directly. You need to connect the device on which you use the app to the Internet to upload the images or videos you capture, and the larger the upload, the longer the transfer to Facebook will take. You also transfer more data if you are uploading longer videos. Videos uploaded via your carrier network and not Wi-Fi will also use data from your monthly quota, so a Wi-Fi connection is often a cheaper option too. You can add comments to the media you shoot and upload with the app, as well as tag friends and add location information before uploading.

Take and Upload Photos with the Facebook App

1 Tap **Photo** on your news feed.

2 Tap **Take Photo or Video**.

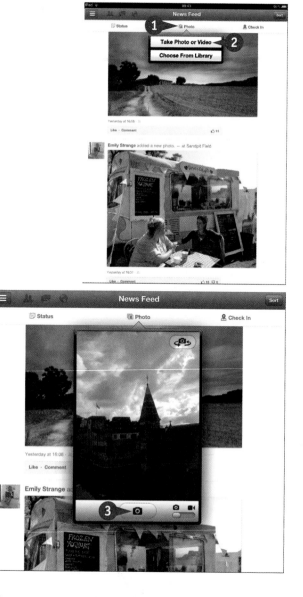

A photo preview window appears.

3 Point the device at your subject, and press the **Camera** button (📷) to take a photo.

A preview of your photo appears.

4 Tap **Use**.

5 Tap anywhere on the image and type a name into the Search box to add tags to the image.

6 Tap **Attach**.

7 Type a comment into the **Say something about this** section.

8 Add a location to your image by tapping **Location** (📍).

9 Tap **Post**.

Facebook adds the photo to your timeline, and it appears on the news feeds of your friends.

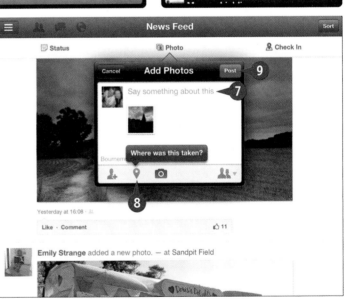

TIPS

Who can see images I take and share with the Facebook app?
You can select who can see your photos by using the **Audience Selector** button (👥) when you post your images.

Can I upload videos with the Facebook app?
Yes. You can change from photo to video mode on the photo preview screen and record a video in the same way you take a photo. You upload the video in the same way as photos, but it may take longer.

Upload Photos on Your Device with the Facebook App

You can upload photos on your mobile device to Facebook from within the Facebook app. You can upload photos in batches, tag friends in them, and add location information as well. The Audience Selector feature works the same as on the Facebook site, allowing you to specify who can see the images you upload. You need an Internet connection to upload your images to Facebook from the app.

Upload Photos on Your Device with the Facebook App

1 On your news feed, tap **Photo.**

2 Tap **Choose From Library**.

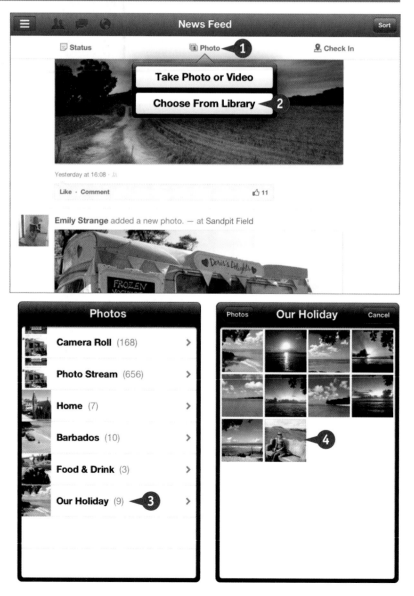

The Photo Library for your device appears.

3 Tap **Camera Roll, Photo Stream** or the title of any albums you have created.

Note: On the original iPad without a camera, this album is called Saved Photos.

Your photos appear.

4 Tap the photo you want to upload.

A preview of your photo appears.

 Tap anywhere on the photo to tag a person.

5 Tap **Attach**.

6 Type a comment in the space above your image.

Ⓑ Tap **Location** (📍) to add a location.

7 Tap **Post**.

The app uploads your photo to Facebook.

TIP

Can I upload more than one photo with the Facebook app?
Yes. After you have selected your first photo, you can tap the **camera** button next to the Location button on the Add Photos window. Two buttons appear below your existing image, allowing you to either take a photo or choose one from your library. Tapping either button allows you to add a new image to your upload. You can continue this process until you have attached all of the pictures you want to upload.

Use the Facebook Messenger App

The Facebook Messenger app is available for Apple iOS, Android, and Blackberry devices and provides a convenient way to send Facebook messages from your phone or tablet. The app is free and you can download it from the app store for your device. Facebook Messenger shows all of your Facebook messages and allows you to begin or continue conversations as well as chat with a group. When you have a connection to the Internet, the app can also notify you when it receives a new message.

Use the Facebook Messenger App

Log In to Your Account

1 Launch the app and type your Facebook login details into the fields provided.

2 Tap **Log In to Facebook**.

Note: If you are already signed in to Facebook, it may simply ask you to click **Continue**.

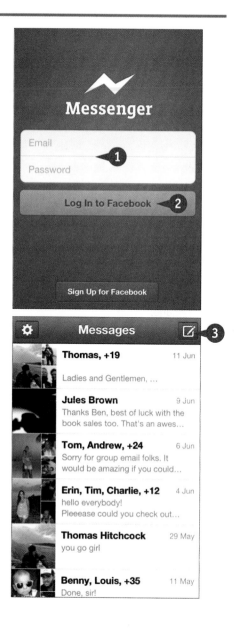

Your previous messages appear.

Start a Conversation

3 Tap **New Message** () at the top right of the screen.

A list of your friends appears.

4 Tap the name of a friend to send him or her a message.

Note: You can also chat with multiple friends by tapping **Group Conversation**.

Cancel	**New Message**
Q Search	
+👥 Group Conversation	>
Thomas Hitchcock ◀ **4**	
Floyd Simmons on mobile	📱
Jon Newman on mobile	📱
Adam Trehane	
Raquel Keegan	
Stuart Tarrant	
More Online Friends	
Georgie **Fletcher**	●

5 Type your message into the field at the bottom of the screen.

A Tap **Camera** (📷) to add a photo.

B Tap **Location** (✈) to add your location.

6 Tap **Send** to send your message.

Your message is sent to the recipient you selected.

< **Back** **Thomas Hitchcock** •••

Ben Harvell 29 May
Was debating with Scott R about creating a shared calendar for all food festivals in the area!

Thomas Hitchcock 29 May
lets do it

Thomas Hitchcock 29 May
keen

A 📷 Drinks again this Friday? ◀**5** ✈ **B** **Send** ◀**6**

TIPS

Can I use another app while I wait for a response to my message?
Yes. You can turn notifications on within the settings section of your device and within the Messenger app. As long as the app is running, you are notified when you receive a new message.

How do I know which of my friends are online?
Only friends who have chat enabled and are logged in to Facebook appear within the app. If they are using a mobile device, a mobile phone image appears next to their name.

Use the Facebook Camera App

amera is an official Facebook app for iPhone users, and is available from the iTunes App Store. The app is free to download and allows you to view photos from friends on Facebook in one place. You can also take photos with the app and select images from your iPhone Camera Roll to upload. You can upload photos in groups, and apply crops and filters to enhance them before they reach Facebook. You can also add comments to photos as well as tags and location information.

Use the Facebook Camera App

1 Launch the Camera app and type your Facebook login details into the fields that appear.

2 Tap **Log In to Facebook**.

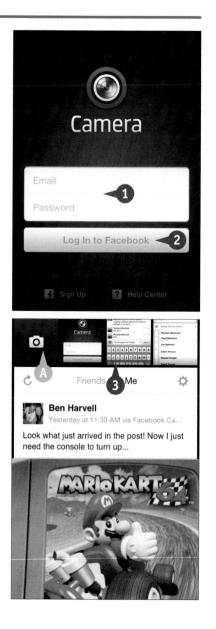

Images from your news feed appear, as well as your own photos.

Ⓐ To take a new photo, tap **Camera** (◉) at the top left of the interface.

3 Tap one of your photos at the top of the screen.

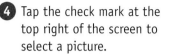

The photo appears.

④ Tap the check mark at the top right of the screen to select a picture.

⑤ Swipe your finger across the screen to view more images.

Note: You can also tap **Grid View** (▦) at the bottom left of the screen to view all your photos on one screen.

⑥ Tap **Create a post** (🖼).

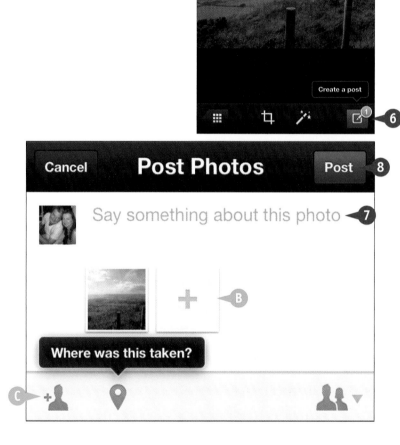

⑦ Type a comment for your photo into the **Say something about this photo** field.

Ⓑ Tap **Add** (➕) to add more images.

Ⓒ You can add friends and locations using the buttons at the bottom of the interface.

⑧ Tap **Post**.

The photos you selected are uploaded to Facebook and appear on your timeline.

Can I view photos from friends with the Facebook Camera app?

Yes. The first screen that appears shows photos that your friends have uploaded, as well as likes and comments on them. If there is more than one photo in a post, you can swipe across them to view more photos.

Can I edit photos within the Facebook Camera app?

Yes. When you select a photo, there are two buttons at the bottom of the screen that allow you to apply filters to the image and crop the photo.

Activate Facebook Text Messages

You can set Facebook to send SMS messages to your mobile phone to notify you of various events related to your account. Depending on your settings, you can receive text messages on your phone telling you when someone has added a comment on a post you have made or on your timeline. It can also inform you when somebody adds you as a friend or confirms your friend request, or you can simply receive a message when any notification occurs. To use Facebook text messaging, you need to first set up the service with your mobile phone number.

Activate Facebook Text Messages

1 Click **Home**.

2 Click the **Account menu** ▾.

3 Click **Account Settings** from the options menu.

4 Click **Mobile**.

5 Click **+ Add a Phone**.

A password window appears.

6 Type your password into the field.

7 Click **Submit**.

The first activation window appears.

8 Click here and select your country and carrier from the pop-up menus.

9 Click **Next**.

The second activation window appears.

⑩ Follow the on-screen instructions for your carrier.

⑪ Click **Next**.

Activate Facebook Texts (Step 2 of 2)

⑩ ➤ 1 Text the letter **F** to **32665 (FBOOK)**

2 When you receive a confirmation code, enter it here:

bnczz|

Facebook doesn't charge for this service. Standard messaging rates apply.

☑ Share my phone number with my friends
☑ Allow friends to text me from Facebook

⑪ ➤ **Next** | **Cancel**

Facebook texts are activated for your phone.

Ⓐ Click **Edit** next to **Notifications** to turn text notifications on and off.

Ⓑ Click **Edit** next to **Facebook Messages** to set which notifications you receive via SMS.

Ⓒ Click **Edit** next to **Daily Text Limit** to set the maximum number of texts you receive each day.

facebook | Search for people, places and things | Ben Harvell Find Friends Home ▾

- General
- Security
- Notifications
- Subscribers
- Apps
- Mobile
- Payments
- Facebook Ads

Mobile Settings

Your phones:
0 751.535.2839 on O2 - Text Activated - Remove
+ Add another mobile phone number

Lose your phone?

Already received a confirmation code?
Confirmation code | **Confirm**

You can also visit your privacy settings or edit your timeline to control who sees the info there.

Text Messaging	Send texts to: 0 751.535.2839	Edit
Notifications	Text notifications are turned off	Edit ◀ Ⓐ
Facebook Messages	Text me: When someone sends me a Message on web or mobile	Ⓑ ▶ Edit
Daily Text Limit	Maximum number of texts Unlimited	Edit ◀ Ⓒ
Post-By-Email Address	Email a photo or video to honk179toque@m.facebook.com and it will be automatically posted to Facebook. Learn about your post-by-email address.	Refresh

Learn more about using Facebook on your phone at Facebook Mobile.

Can I specify when I receive messages on my mobile phone from Facebook?
Yes. Under the Mobile Settings section of the Account Settings screen, you can set a period of time when you do not receive messages, such as at night.

Will I still receive messages even when I am using Facebook?
Yes. You will continue to receive messages from Facebook even if you are logged into your account. However, within the Mobile Settings screen, you can opt to stop messages when you are logged in to your account.

Upload Photos to Facebook via E-Mail

Each Facebook account has a unique Post-By-Email address that allows you to send e-mails with attachments to Facebook. The attachments that you send in these e-mails are uploaded to your Facebook account, and you can include comments for the photo or video you attach by adding one to the e-mail subject line. You can view your Post-By-Email address within the Mobile Settings screen for your account, and it also appears when you log in to Facebook Mobile from a browser on your mobile device and tap **Photo.**

Upload Photos to Facebook via E-Mail

Locate Your Post-By-Email Address

1. Click **Home.**

2. Click the **Account menu** [▾].

3. Click **Account Settings** from the options menu.

4. Click **Mobile.**

Ⓐ Your Post-By-Email Address appears here.

Upload Photos and Videos by E-Mail

5. Create a new e-mail on your device and attach a photo to it.

6. Add your Post-By-Email address to the To: field of your e-mail.

7. Add a comment for your photo in the subject line of the e-mail.

When you send your e-mail, the attachment is uploaded to Facebook with any comments you included.

Access Your Mobile Timeline

You can view the timeline display on your Facebook account on mobile devices. The mobile timeline condenses into a single column and shows all of your posts, likes, photos, and life events. You can change your timeline cover image using Facebook Mobile and also remove posts from your timeline. These changes appear across your Facebook account on all platforms.

Access Your Mobile Timeline

1 Visit **m.facebook.com** on your mobile device.

Note: You may need to log in to your account.

2 Tap the button at the top left of the page to reveal the left pane.

3 Tap your name.

Your mobile timeline appears.

Ⓐ Tap the **Camera** button (📷) to take or upload a new cover image.

Ⓑ Tap **Update Status** to write a new status message.

Ⓒ Tap **Check In** to check in to a new location.

Ⓓ Swipe across posts from right to left and tap the **Delete** ⊗ to delete them.

Set Up Instagram to Post Facebook Photos

Instagram, which is owned by Facebook, offers a convenient way to upload images from your mobile device to your Facebook account. The app provides a number of filters to enhance photos you take, and you can also select images to share that you already have on your device. To send Instagram photos to Facebook, you must first log in to Instagram via the free Instagram app and allow it permission to post images to Facebook. Once you have set it up, you can select whether or not to share a photo on Facebook once you have taken it.

Set Up Instagram to Post Facebook Photos

1 Tap **Settings** (▣) at the bottom right of the interface.

2 Tap **Edit sharing settings.**

3 Tap **Facebook.**

Note: If you are logged in to the Facebook mobile app, the Facebook window appears. Otherwise, you must type in your Facebook account details via the mobile web interface.

Profile	Sharing Settings
○ Twitter	>
○ Facebook ◀③	>
○ Flickr	>
○ Tumblr	>
○ Foursquare	>

4 Tap **Okay.**

When you take a photo, you now see an option to upload the image to Facebook.

Cancel	facebook	Okay ◀④

Instagram
Fast, beautiful photo sharing

Already Authorized

You have already authorized this app. Press Okay to continue.

About this app

A fast, beautiful and fun way to share your photos with friends and family.

By proceeding, you also agree to Instagram's Terms of Service and Privacy Policy.

TIPS

How do I share photos to Facebook from the Instagram app?
Once you have allowed Instagram access to your Facebook account, an on/off Facebook toggle appears in the sharing section of the screen that appears when you take a photo with the Instagram app. Setting this option to **On** and tapping the **Done** button sends your photo to Facebook.

How do I log in to the Instagram app?
When you first launch the Instagram app, you have the option to log in or sign up. If you do not already have an Instagram account, tap the **Sign Up** button. If not, tap the **Login** button.

CHAPTER 14

Using Location Services on Facebook

You can check in to locations and share them on Facebook; add locations to posts, photos, and videos; and join networks on Facebook.

Check In to a Location with the Facebook App

Using the Facebook app on a mobile device, you can check in to locations you visit. The app shares this information with your friends on Facebook. You need to connect your mobile device to a mobile network or Wi-Fi in order for check-ins to work, and the device also needs to determine your location using GPS. You may also need to activate location services on your device. Make sure to use the correct privacy settings using the **Audience Selector** when posting your location to Facebook for additional safety.

Check In to a Location with the Facebook App

1 On the Facebook app home page, tap **Check In**.

Note: Your device may ask you for permission to use your current location.

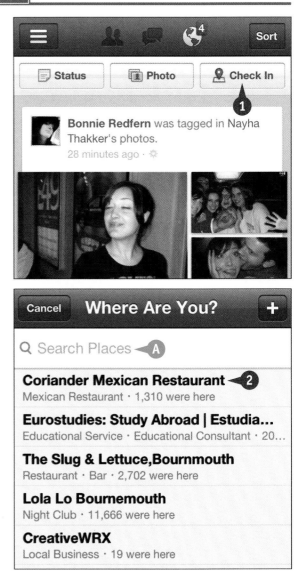

A list of nearby locations appears.

Ⓐ If you cannot find your location, you can search for it by typing into the **Search Places** field.

2 Tap the name of your current location.

The Facebook app adds your location to the comment field.

3 Type a comment using the on-screen keyboard.

B You can also add people and images to your check-in by tapping the buttons at the bottom of the screen.

C You can select who can see your check-in by using the **Audience Selector** (👥).

4 Tap **Post**.

Your check-in now appears on your timeline and on the news feeds of your friends.

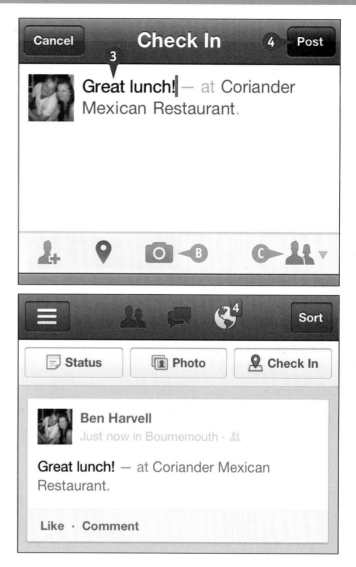

TIPS

What if I do not see my location?
If you search for your location and still cannot find it, you can create one to check in to by tapping the **Add** link below the Search box.

Why do I see multiple listings for my location?
Because anyone can create a location, you may encounter multiple instances of one place. The number of check-ins at each location appears below its name, so it is usually best to select the location with the most check-ins.

Add Your Location to a Facebook Post

When you post an update to Facebook, you can include a location that is visible to anyone who you allow to see your post. This information also appears on your Facebook map, which appears on your timeline. You can type any location into the Location field when you update your status, and a list of options appears. From this list, you can select the correct location or, if you do not see your location, you can add a new location to Facebook.

Add Your Location to a Facebook Post

1. Click **Home.**
2. Click **Update Status.**
3. Type your status message in the Status field.
4. Click the **location** button.

5. Type your current location into the **Where are you?** field.

   A list appears of possible locations.

6. Click your location in the list.

   Your location now appears in your status update.

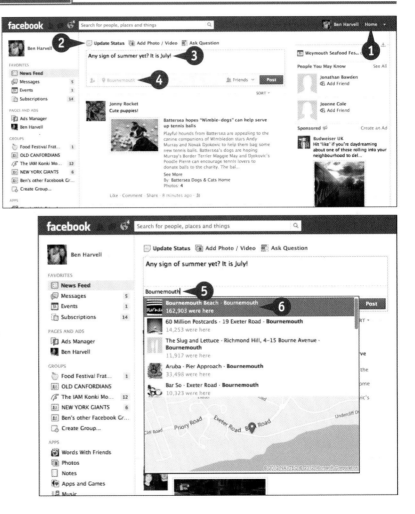

Add Locations to Videos

CHAPTER 14

Like photos, check-ins, and status updates, you can add a location to videos posted on Facebook. You can add location information to any video you have permission to edit on Facebook and also create a new location if none of the recommendations made by Facebook match the location you want to add. You can add location information to videos from the Edit Video screen, and the information appears below the video title on Facebook.

Add Locations to Videos

1 Click **Edit** below the information for your video.

The Edit Video page appears.

2 Type a location into the **Where** field.

3 Click a location on the list that appears.

4 Click **Save**.

Facebook adds the location to your video.

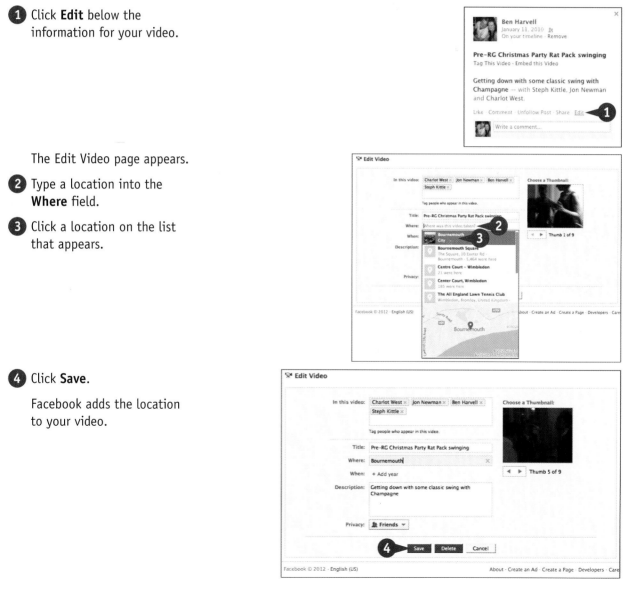

261

Add Locations to Photos

You can add locations to photos on Facebook that do not already have location information included. Most mobile phones and some cameras embed location data to photos you take, and Facebook can make use of that information when you upload pictures to your account. For those photos without location information, you can use the options menu found below Facebook photos in the photo viewer. Clicking Add Location on the options menu allows you to type a location and select the correct place from a list of suggestions, or create a new location on Facebook.

Add Locations to Photos

1 Click a photo on Facebook.

The photo appears.

2 Click **Options**.

3 Click **Add Location** from the options menu.

4 Type a location into the **Where was this photo taken?** field.

5 Click the location from the list that appears.

6 Click **Done Editing**.

Facebook adds the location to your photo.

Which photos can I add a location to?
You can add a location to any photos you have uploaded or are tagged in, as long as they do not already have a location assigned to them. You can also add a location to photos uploaded by friends if they have allowed it.

What if the location does not appear on the list?
You can add a location by typing a name for it into the **Where was this photo taken?** field and clicking the **Add** link.

Change or Update a Story Location

You can change the location information that appears below a story you have added to Facebook, whether it is a status update, photo, or other event on your timeline. This feature allows you to adjust the location if it is incorrect. Clicking the Edit button next to almost all stories you have added to your timeline allows you to change or add the location. The Change Location (or Add Location) window then allows you to type in a new location and select the correct place from the list that appears.

Change or Update a Story Location

1 Click **Edit** (⬛) on the story you want to add a location to.

2 Click **Change Location** from the options menu.

Note: If there is not yet a location for the image, the button may say **Add Location.**

The Change Location window appears.

3 Type a location into the field.

4 Click a location from the list that appears.

5 Click **Okay.**

Facebook adds the new location to the story.

View the Page for a Location

Each location you add to a story, photo, or video on Facebook has its own page. Clicking a location beneath a story takes you to that page and also shows information about the location, such as nearby businesses, Wikipedia information, and friends who have worked or visited there. Some locations may show a page instead of a location, which allows you to like the place you have visited and receive updates from the owner of the page.

View the Page for a Location

1 Click a location that appears below a status update, photo, or check-in.

The page for the location appears.

A Businesses and other places within this location appear here.

B You can find more information on the location by clicking **Info** or **Wikipedia**.

C Friends who have liked, worked, or checked in at this location appear on the right side of the page.

Share a Location on Facebook

You can share locations on Facebook with either some or all of your friends, or simply share to your own timeline. Sharing a location on Facebook allows others to see information about the location, and is useful when researching holidays and other getaways. Places on Facebook include an options button from which you can choose to share the location or add it to your Interest Lists or Favorites for your Facebook page.

Share a Location on Facebook

1 Click the **Action** menu () on the Facebook page for the location you want to share.

Note: You can find location pages by using the Search box or by clicking a location below a post on Facebook.

2 Click **Share** from the options menu.

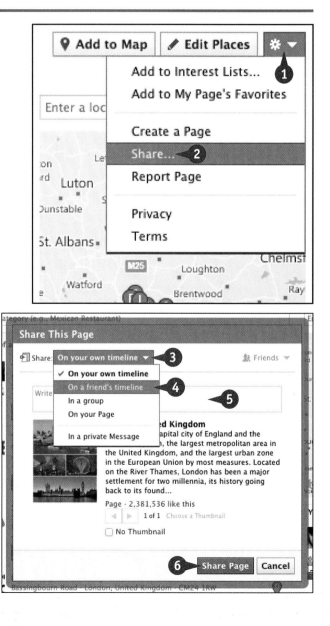

The Share This Page window appears.

3 Click the **Share** menu.

4 Click where you want to share the page.

5 Type a message into the **Write something** field.

6 Click **Share Page**.

Facebook shares the page to the location you selected.

Add a Location to Your Map

You can add locations to the map that appears on your Facebook timeline. The map updates whenever you check in to a location or add a location to a status update or photo, and you can also choose to add a location at any time from the location page, including information about who you were with and when you visited the location. Facebook then adds this information to your map, and the group you select with the Audience Selector can view it.

Add a Location to Your Map

1 Click **Add to Map** on a location page.

2 Type information about your visit to the location in the **Write something** field.

A Click **When were you here?** to add a date you visited the location.

B Click **With** to tag people in your visit to the location.

C Click the **Friends Audience Selector** () to choose who can see the location on your map.

3 Click **Post.**

The location appears on your timeline and on your map.

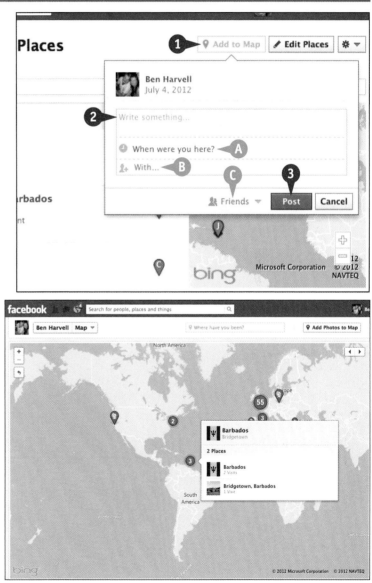

Join a Network on Facebook

Networks on Facebook are for students at educational institutions, members of organizations, and employees at companies that Facebook recognizes. In order to access a network, you need to provide an e-mail address for the institution the network is associated with, such as your university e-mail address. You can join up to five different networks on Facebook and set one primary network. This is useful for students on an exchange with a different school or graduates who want to remain part of their school network and also join the network of their employer.

Join a Network on Facebook

1 Click **Home.**

2 Click the **Account** menu ([·]).

3 Click **Account Settings** from the options menu.

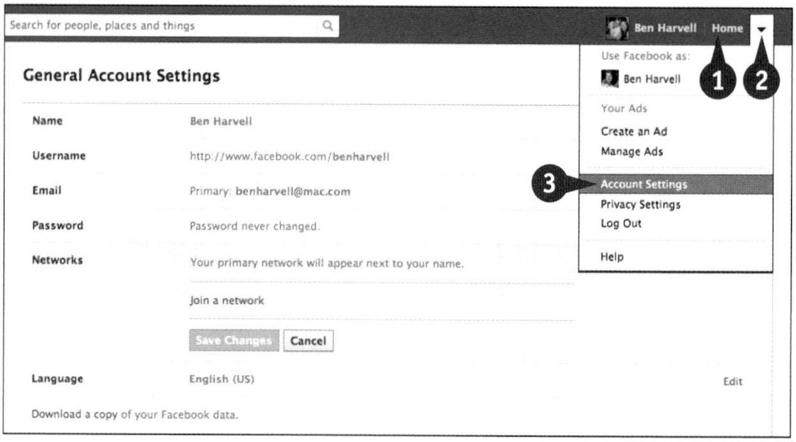

Search for people, places and things | Ben Harvell Home

General Account Settings

Use Facebook as:
Ben Harvell

Name	Ben Harvell
Username	http://www.facebook.com/benharvell
Email	Primary: benharvell@mac.com
Password	Password never changed.
Networks	Your primary network will appear next to your name.

Your Ads
Create an Ad
Manage Ads

Account Settings
Privacy Settings
Log Out

Help

Join a network

Save Changes Cancel

| Language | English (US) | Edit |

Download a copy of your Facebook data.

4 Click **Networks.**

5 Click **Join a network.**

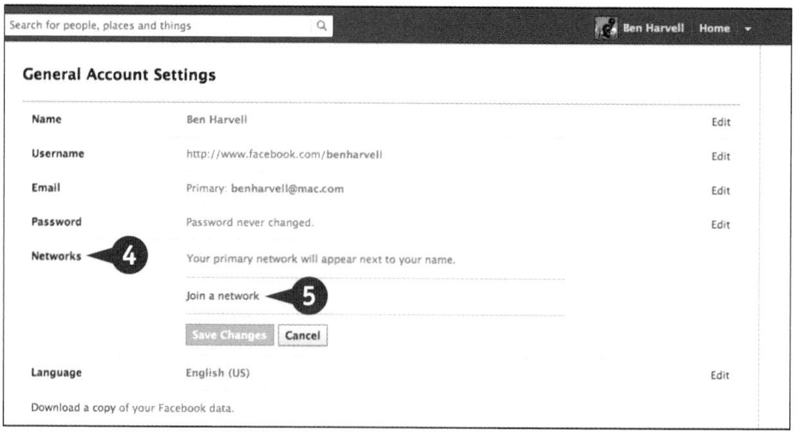

Search for people, places and things | Ben Harvell Home

General Account Settings

Name	Ben Harvell	Edit
Username	http://www.facebook.com/benharvell	Edit
Email	Primary: benharvell@mac.com	Edit
Password	Password never changed.	Edit
Networks	Your primary network will appear next to your name.	

Join a network

Save Changes Cancel

| Language | English (US) | Edit |

Download a copy of your Facebook data.

6 Type a network name into the **Network name** field.

7 Click a network from the list that appears.

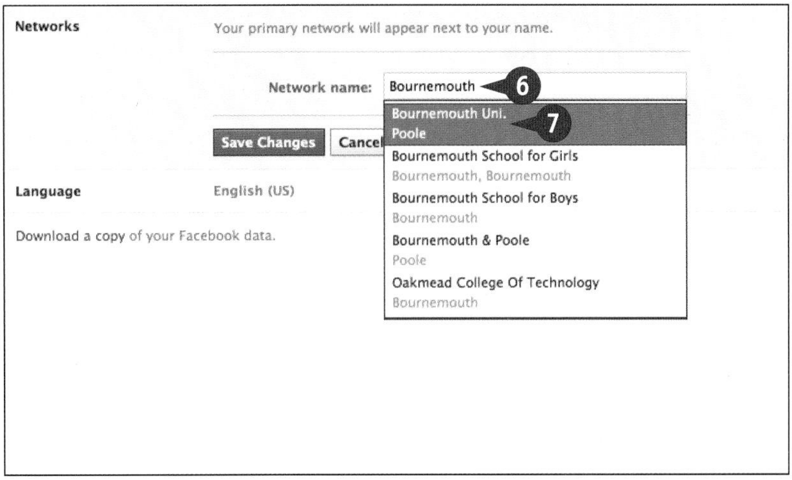

Networks | Your primary network will appear next to your name.

Network name: Bournemouth ◄6

Bournemouth Uni. ◄7
Poole
Bournemouth School for Girls
Bournemouth, Bournemouth
Bournemouth School for Boys
Bournemouth
Bournemouth & Poole
Poole
Oakmead College Of Technology
Bournemouth

Save Changes   Cancel

Language   English (US)

Download a copy of your Facebook data.

8 Type an e-mail address associated with the network you want to join.

9 Click **Save Changes**.

The network is added to your account and appears on your profile.

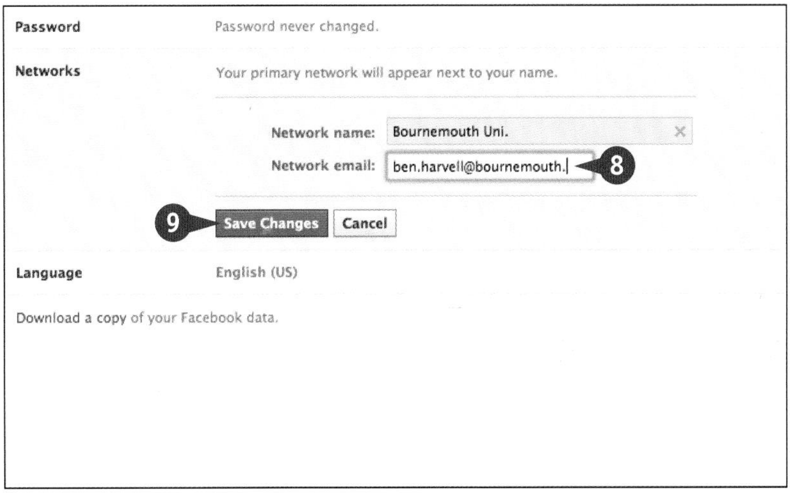

Password   Password never changed.

Networks   Your primary network will appear next to your name.

Network name: Bournemouth Uni.   ✕

Network email: ben.harvell@bournemouth. ◄8

9 Save Changes   Cancel

Language   English (US)

Download a copy of your Facebook data.

TIP

Can I still join my college network if I do not have an e-mail address for my college?
No, Facebook will not allow you to join a college network unless you have an e-mail address associated with it. You need to be able to send and receive e-mail from the address in order to validate it. Contact your college and ask if you are eligible for an e-mail address. If you are eligible, have your college set the e-mail up, so you can join the network for your college.

CHAPTER 15

Understanding Facebook Ads and Pages

You can create your own page for a business or service on Facebook and promote it using the Facebook advertising platform.

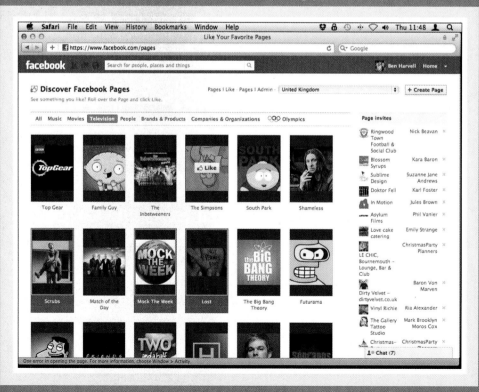

Create a Facebook Page

You can use a Facebook page to promote a business, brand, or service, or an individual group/ organization or charity. A page is different from a standard Facebook account and can be liked by others in order to promote it. Pages include a timeline like a regular Facebook account, and users can promote them with Facebook ads. Setting up a Facebook page requires an existing Facebook user to manage the account in most cases, so ensure you are logged in to your account when you start building your page on Facebook.

Create a Facebook Page

Create a Page

1. Type **www.facebook.com/ pages** into the URL bar of your browser.

2. Click **+ Create Page**.

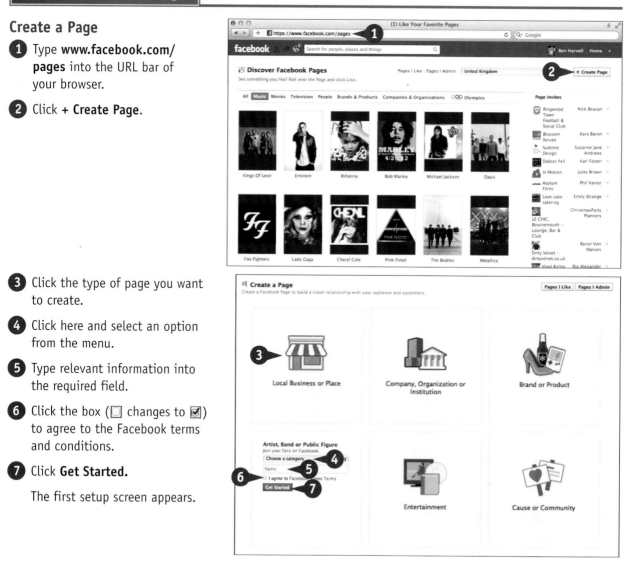

3. Click the type of page you want to create.

4. Click here and select an option from the menu.

5. Type relevant information into the required field.

6. Click the box (☐ changes to ☑) to agree to the Facebook terms and conditions.

7. Click **Get Started.**

   The first setup screen appears.

Upload a Profile Picture to Your Page

8 Click **Upload From Computer.**

A browser window appears.

9 Select a photo for your page from your computer.

10 Click **Choose.**

Facebook uploads your picture.

11 Click **Next.**

continued ▶

TIPS

Can I import images from my own website?

Yes. Instead of clicking the **Upload From Computer** option, click **Import From Website.** Facebook asks you to type the URL of your website. When you have typed your website URL, click the **Import** button. Facebook finds images from your site and shows a preview of each image. Click the image you want to use on your page, and click the **Save Photo** button to set it as the profile picture for your page.

Do I have to add a profile picture at this stage?

No. You can add a profile picture later. If you would rather not upload a profile picture at this point, click the **Skip** button.

etting up a Facebook page is similar to creating a personal Facebook account, as you need to supply a profile picture and basic information. You can also create a unique URL for your Facebook page so that people can quickly find it using a memorable link. Once your page is live, you can begin adding updates, images, and milestones to its timeline in the same way that you would on your personal Facebook page.

Create a Facebook Page (continued)

Add Basic Information

1 Type a description of your product or service into the first field.

2 Type a link to your website, Twitter page, or Yelp link in the second field.

A To add more sites, click **Add Another Site**.

3 Click **Save Info**.

Facebook creates your page.

4 Click the **Invite** button next to the names of friends to invite them to your page.

5 Click the **Hide** button to hide the Admin Panel.

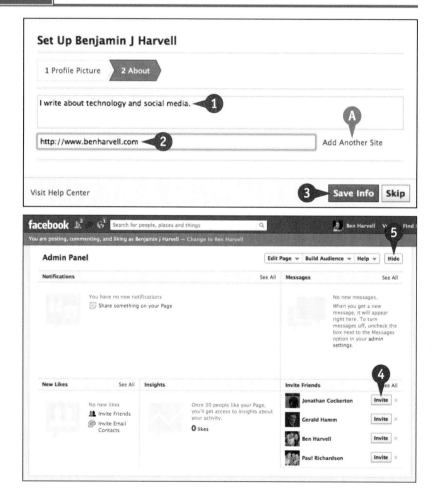

Add a Cover Image

6 Click **Add a Cover**.

7 Click **Upload Photo** from the options menu.

A browser window appears.

8 Select the image you want to use as your page cover.

9 Click **Choose.**

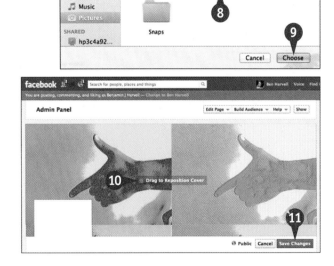

Facebook uploads your cover image.

10 Click and drag the cover image to position it.

11 Click **Save Changes**.

Facebook saves your cover image.

TIPS

Can I change my profile picture?
Yes. Position your cursor over the profile picture area on your page and click the **Edit Profile Picture** button. From here, you can upload a new image, choose an image from your photos, or take a new photo with your webcam.

How do I add new status updates and events to my page?
You can update your status, upload photos and videos, and add events to your timeline in the same way as on your regular Facebook page. A box below your profile picture allows you to perform all of these actions by clicking the relevant option, such as Status or Photo.

Update Your Page Info

The information you add to your page is what sells it, so make sure you include as much information as possible to enlighten and excite page viewers. Editing a page allows you to include contact information, descriptions about you and your product or service, and when it began or was founded. This information is available to anyone who views your page and, if your page is for a physical location, such as a shop or cafe, you can add address details so Facebook users can check in when they visit it.

Update Your Page Info

1 Click **Edit Page** at the top of your Facebook page.

2 Click **Update Info** from the options menu.

A If your page is unofficial and you want to link to the official page, type its URL in this field.

B Click **Add year** and then click the arrows to select the year your business or brand began.

C Click the **Start Type** drop down menu.

D Select what began on this date — that is, when you were born, launched a product, or formed a company.

E Add address details for your page in these fields. This allows others to find your location.

F Add biography information and a short description of the subject of your page in these fields. You can also include awards you have won.

G Select your gender and fill out personal information and interests in these fields.

H Add additional contact information in the final three fields.

3 Click **Save Changes**.

Facebook adds the information you entered to your page.

Can I change the username for my page?
Yes. You can click the **Change Username** link when editing basic information on your page. You may not be allowed to change your username until your page has more fans, however.

Can I change my page type if I change my business or profession?
Yes. You can change the category of your page as well as the institution type by using the two drop down menus at the top of the screen when you are editing your basic information.

View Page Admin and Insights

When you have logged in to your Facebook page, you can access the Admin Panel to view recent notifications such as messages and likes, and also access insight into your page activity. The Insight screen shows the reach of posts on your page and allows you to learn how many people are seeing and interacting with the content on your page. You can also download insight data for your page and store it on your computer for your records.

View Page Admin and Insights

① Click the **Account** menu (⊡).

② Click your page title under the **Use Facebook as:** section of the options menu.

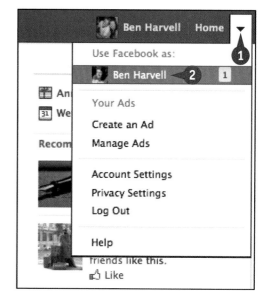

Your page appears.

③ If the Admin Panel for your page does not already appear, click **Show** to display it.

The Admin Panel appears.

④ Click **See All** next to Insights.

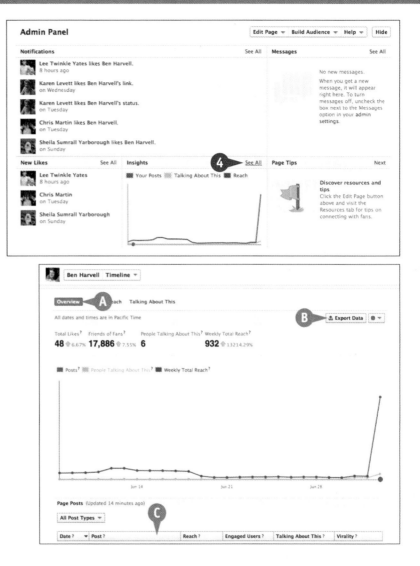

The Insights page appears.

Ⓐ Click the links at the top of the page to view different sets of information.

Ⓑ Click **Export Data** to download a copy of your page Insight data.

Ⓒ Information regarding individual posts appears at the bottom of the page.

TIPS

How can I find out more about Page Insights?
Click the **Options** button at the top right of the screen on the Insights page and click **Page Insights Guide** from the options menu. This opens a PDF file that further explains Page Insight. Depending on your browser, the file may be download to your computer.

Why does my Page Admin Panel look so empty?
If you have only just created your page, then your Admin Panel will not contain much information. As more people like your page, view its content, and send you messages, the Admin Panel will become busier.

Invite People to View Your Page via E-Mail

Promoting your page is essential in order to gain the most likes and enhance interaction with customers or potential clients. You can quickly suggest your page to a number of people at once by inviting them via e-mail. You can log in to your existing e-mail service using Facebook, and access all of the contacts within it in order to choose whom to invite to view your page. You can also upload a contact list from an e-mail client to perform the same task.

Invite People to View Your Page via E-Mail

1. Click **Build Audience**.

2. Click **Invite Email Contacts** from the pop-up menu.

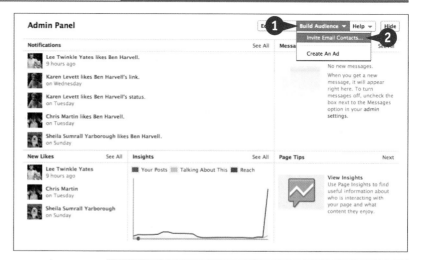

The Invite Email Contacts window appears.

3. Click **Invite Contacts** next to the e-mail service you use.

4. Type your e-mail address and password into the fields that appear.

5. Click **Invite Contacts**.

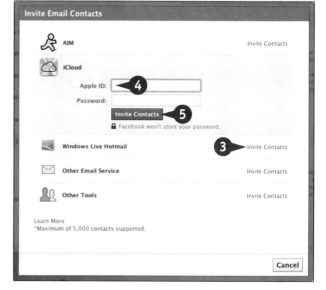

Your contacts are imported and appear on-screen.

6 Click the box next to each contact you want to invite (☐ changes to (☑)).

7 Click **Preview Invitation**.

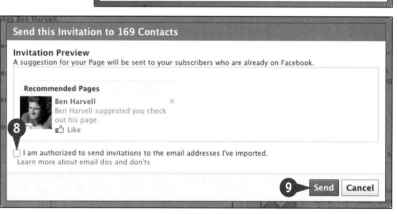

A preview of your invitation appears.

8 Click the box to confirm you are authorized to use these contacts (☐ changes to (☑)).

9 Click **Send**.

Facebook sends your invites via e-mail.

TIPS

Can I upload a contact file to use for invites?
Yes. Click the **Other Tools** section in the Invite Email Contacts window and upload a contact file from Microsoft Outlook Express, Thunderbird, or the Contacts or Address Book app on a Mac linked to Apple Mail. Then click **Upload Contacts** to add your contacts to Facebook and select whomever you would like to invite to view your page.

What if I do not see my e-mail service?
You can either use the **Other Email Service** option in the Invite Email Contacts window or click **Other Tools** and upload a contact file from your e-mail software.

Invite Facebook Friends to View Your Page

As well as contacting people by e-mail, you can use your most valuable asset on Facebook, your friends list, in order to promote your page. Using your personal account, you can invite friends on Facebook to view your page by selecting which of them you want to send an invite to. Friends are often more likely to visit and like your page and therefore spread its reach to more Facebook users.

Invite Facebook Friends to View Your Page

① Access your Facebook page while using Facebook with your personal account.

② Click **Build Audience.**

③ Click **Invite Friends** from the options menu.

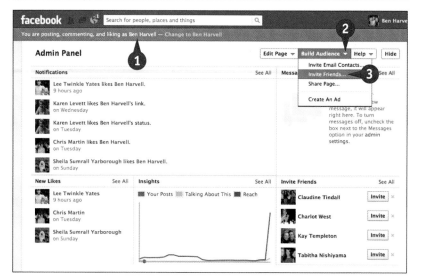

The Suggest to friends window appears.

④ Click the box next to each friend you want to suggest your page to (☐ changes to ☑).

⑤ Click **Submit.**

Facebook suggests your page to the friends you chose.

Adjust Notification Settings for Your Page

B y default, Facebook notifies you by e-mail when there is activity on your Facebook page. This could be a person liking your page, adding a comment, or sending a message. Should your page see a lot of activity, you may begin to receive a lot of notifications each day. If you do not want to receive these notifications by e-mail, you can turn page notifications on or off from within the settings section of your page.

Adjust Notification Settings for Your Page

1 Click **Edit Page.**

2 Click **Update Info** from the options menu.

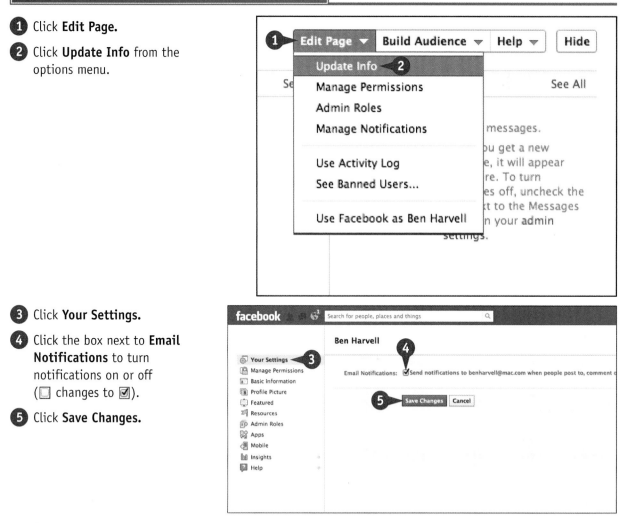

3 Click **Your Settings.**

4 Click the box next to **Email Notifications** to turn notifications on or off (☐ changes to ☑).

5 Click **Save Changes.**

Add a Featured Owner to Your Page

Page owners administer a Facebook page and can be showcased as a Featured Page Owner on that page. From the page settings screen, you can specify which of the administrators of a page you want to set as Featured Page Owners, and you can include yourself as a Featured Page Owner as well. When you make a person a Featured Page Owner, his or her information appears under the About section of your page.

Add a Featured Owner to Your Page

1 Click **Edit Page**.

2 Click **Update Info** from the options menu.

The settings screen appears.

3 Click **Featured.**

4 Click **Add Featured Page Owners**.

The Edit Featured Page Owners window appears.

5 Click the box next to your name on the list (☐ changes to ☑).

6 Click **Save**.

Facebook adds you as a Featured Page Owner.

Like a Page on Facebook

Liking a page on Facebook signals your appreciation of its content or the institution it stands for. This could be a person or a business or a charitable, social, or service organization. When you like a page, Facebook automatically subscribes you to its updates, which appear on your news feed. Your Like also appears on your timeline and news feed, and on the news feeds of your friends. You may also appear on the page you have liked or in ads for that page.

Like a Page on Facebook

1 Type the name of the page you want to like into the search pane at the top of the Facebook interface.

2 Click the name of the page within the search results.

The page appears.

3 Click **Like**.

The Like button changes to Liked and the Like appears on your timeline.

Create a Facebook Ad to Promote Your Page

Facebook has its own advertising platform that allows you to promote services among Facebook users. If you already have a Facebook page, you can pay to promote it across Facebook with a small advertisement that appears on the right side of the Facebook interface. There are a number of different advertising styles on Facebook, and you can adapt the text and image for your ad, and preview it before it goes live.

Create a Facebook Ad to Promote Your Page

1 Type **www.facebook.com/ advertising** into the URL bar of your browser.

2 Click **Create an Ad.**

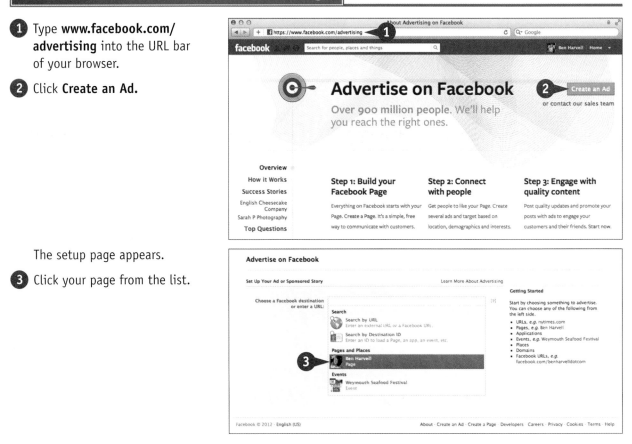

The setup page appears.

3 Click your page from the list.

④ Click the name of your page under the **What do you want to promote?** section.

⑤ Click **A new ad about** under the **People will see:** section.

⑥ Type the main body of your ad in the **Text** field.

⑦ Click here and choose where you want the ad to link to from the pop-up menu.

A preview of your ad appears at the right side of the screen.

Can I change the image for my ad?
Yes. By default, the ad uses the profile picture for your page, but you can change the image by clicking the **Choose File** button under the **Image** section or clicking the **Select from image library** link.

What is the difference between an ad and a sponsored story?
A sponsored story allows you to promote news feed stories about interactions people have had with your brand, product, or service. If a person likes or comments on your page, that interaction may appear as a sponsored story on the news feeds of their friends.

When you create a Facebook ad campaign, you can specify the audience you want to target with your ad. This could be people of a certain age group or gender, or those who have liked other pages that are similar to yours. You can also set a budget for your ad campaign to specify how much you are willing to spend per day or in total in order to promote your page.

Create a Facebook Ad to Promote Your Page (continued)

Set a Target Audience for Your Ad

1 Scroll down to the **Choose Your Audience** section and type the locations you want to target with your ad into the **Location** field.

2 Click here and select an age range you want to target with your ad from the pop-up menus.

3 Select the gender you are targeting with your ad from the **Gender** section.

4 Type the precise interests of your target audience into the **Precise Interests** field and click other categories in the **Broad Categories** section.

5 Click the type of connections you want to target from the Connections section.

The audience information for your ad updates on the right side of the page.

Note: If the audience is too small, consider changing some of your targeting settings.

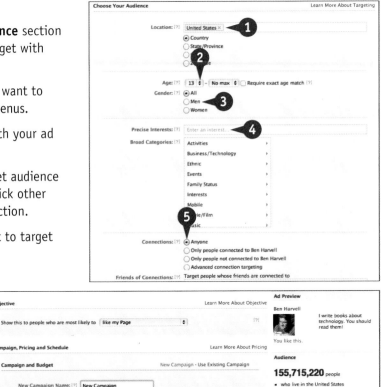

288

Set an Objective and Budget for Your Ad

6 Click the menu under the **Objective** section and select who to show your ad to.

7 Type a name for your ad campaign in the **New Campaign Name** field.

8 Type the amount that you want to use as a budget for your ad into the **Campaign Budget** field.

9 Click here and select whether you want to use your budget per day or as a whole from the pop-up menu.

10 Click the box under **Campaign Schedule** to begin running the campaign continuously once you have paid for it.

11 Click **Place Order**.

Your ad is ordered, and Facebook will review it before approving and publishing it.

Objective   Learn More About Objective

Show this to people who are most likely to   like my Page   **6**

Campaign, Pricing and Schedule   Learn More About Pricing

Campaign and Budget   New Campaign - Use Existing Campaign

New Campaign Name: New Campaign **7**

Campaign Budget: 10   Per day **8** **9**

Campaign Schedule: ☑ Run my campaign continuously starting today

Pricing: ...will be charged every time someone sees your ad ...onsored story (CPM) because you have chosen an ...tive other than "clicks". **10**

11 Place Order   Review Ad

By clicking the "Place Order" button, I agree to the Facebook Statement of Rights and Responsibilities including my obligation to comply with the Facebook Advertising Guidelines. I understand that failure to comply with the Terms and Conditions and the Advertising Guidelines may result in a variety of consequences, including the cancellation of any advertisements I have placed, and termination of my account. I understand that if I am resident or have my principal place of business in the US or Canada, I am contracting solely with Facebook, Inc. Otherwise I am contracting solely with Facebook Ireland Limited.

Ad Preview

Ben Harvell

I write books about technology. You should read them!

You like this.

Audience

155,715,220 people

• who live in the United States

Ads and Pages

Your ad was created successfully.
It will start running after it is approved, which can take up to 24 hours. Please check back once your ad is approved to monitor its performance. You can also edit your creative, or change targeting and delivery information below at any time.

Account
Ben Harvell ▾

All Campaigns ›

Campaigns & Ads
  All Ads
  Pages
  Reports
  Settings
  Billing
  Power Editor

Help
Learn More

Search your ads

Campaign: Page Promotion   Create an Ad

European Union Customers: Facebook needs to ensure your tax information is correct in order to properly determine the application of Irish Value Added Tax ("VAT")
Please take a moment to update your VAT information.

Campaign Name   Status   Budget   Duration (Pacific Time)
Page Promotion ✎   ▶ Active ✎ $10.00 ✎ Daily   07/05/2012 3:41am - Ongoing ✎

Audience   Response

Targeted
Reach
Social Reach   ■ Clicks ■ Actions

No ads in this campaign received impressions in the past 28 days, so there is no audience data to display.

06/11 06/14 06/17 06/23 06/23 06/26 06/29 07/02

Last 7 Days ▾   All Except Deleted ▾   Select rows to edit   Full Report   1 result ◄ ►

TIPS

Can I preview my ad before I order it?

Yes. Click the **Review Ad** button before you click the **Place Order** button to see how your ad will look and whom it will be targeting.

How can I target a more specific audience?

Click the **Show advanced targeting options** link within the **Choose Your Audience** section when you create your ad. This section allows you to determine whether you target people in a particular type of relationship (married, single, engaged), education status, and sexual orientation.

Hide Ads on Your News Feed

I f you are frequently seeing advertisements next to your news feed that you do not like, are not interested in, or find offensive, you can hide them. When you hide an ad, you are less likely to see it again, and you can tell Facebook why you hid the ad in order to provide feedback on your preferences. When you hide an ad on Facebook, it disappears and a different ad replaces it.

Hide Ads on Your News Feed

1 Click **Home.**

2 Click **News Feed.**

3 Position your cursor over the ad you want to hide.

An **X** appears at the top right of the ad.

4 Click the **X.**

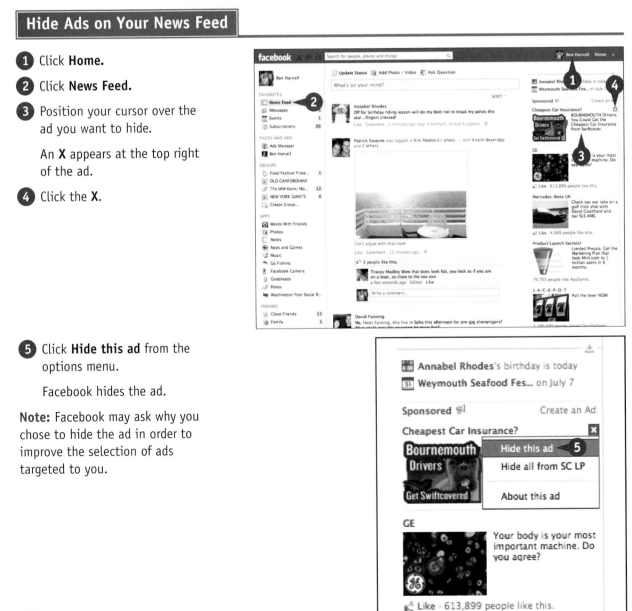

5 Click **Hide this ad** from the options menu.

Facebook hides the ad.

Note: Facebook may ask why you chose to hide the ad in order to improve the selection of ads targeted to you.

Add Page Likes to Improve Ads That You See

If you are seeing ads on Facebook that don't interest you, you can improve the accuracy of ads that you see by liking more pages on Facebook. Ads are targeted toward Facebook users who fit particular criteria and, as a result, the more information Facebook knows about what you like and choose not to like, the more suitable the ads you see will be. You can like a number of pages quickly by visiting the Facebook Pages page and clicking any of the pages that appear in order to like them.

Add Page Likes to Improve Ads That You See

1 Type **www.facebook.com/ pages** into the URL bar of your browser.

The Discover Facebook Pages page appears.

A Click a category to view different page types.

B Pages you have been invited to appear on the right.

2 Click a page that interests you to like it.

The page title and image are highlighted in blue.

Note: To unlike a page you have liked, click it a second time.

Manage Your Ad Campaigns

When you have created an ad campaign on Facebook, you can monitor its progress and make changes at any time. Using the Manage Ads option from the account menu, you can view the reach of your ad, how many people have clicked your ad, and how much you are paying for your campaign. When you generate these reports, you can download them to your computer as a *CSV* file, which stands for comma-separated values. These files can be opened in a number of applications from text editors to spreadsheet tools like Excel. You can also pause campaigns or cancel them completely from the campaign report screen.

Manage Your Ad Campaigns

1 Click the **Account** menu ([·]).

2 Click **Manage Ads** from the options menu.

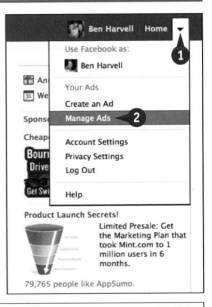

Your ad campaigns appear.

3 Click the title of an ad campaign.

The campaign report appears.

Ⓐ A chart denotes the audience for your campaign.

Ⓑ The response to your campaign appears on a graph.

Ⓒ Detailed reporting, including clicks and reach, appear at the bottom of the screen.

④ Click **Full Report**.

The View Advertising Report screen appears.

Ⓓ Click **Export Report** to download your report as a CSV file.

⑤ Type dates into the **Date Range** field to set a period of time for your report.

TIPS

How can I see how much I am spending on Facebook ads?

When you are managing your ad campaigns, click **Billing** on the left side of the screen to show your current bill, and when and how much Facebook will charge you.

How do I stop an ad campaign?

Click the arrow in the Status column for the campaign you want to stop. Click **Paused** or **Deleted** from the options menu to temporarily suspend the campaign or remove it completely.

Index